MARDUKITE MASTER COURSE
ACADEMY LECTURES
VOL. 3

MESOPOTAMIAN TRADITION

Titles in this series by Joshua Free:
Vol.1 – Magick & Mysticism
Vol.2 – Druids, Elves & Dragons
Vol.3 – Mesopotamian Tradition
Vol.4 – Mardukite Systemology

Mardukite Research Library Catlogue No. "MMC-2M"

Based on the Lectures by Joshua Free for the
Mardukite Master Course given during September 2020
excerpted from *The Complete Mardukite Master Course*

Every effort has been given to match wording and inflection for lecture transcripts based on the recordings made by Mardukite Academy of Systemology

Published from
Mardukite Borsippa HQ, San Luis Valley, Colorado

cum superiorum privilegio veniaque

The Founding Church of Mardukite Zuism,
Mardukite Academy & Systemology Society

MARDUKITE ACADEMY — COLLECTOR'S EDITION

MARDUKITE MASTER COURSE ACADEMY LECTURES VOL. 3

MESOPOTAMIAN TRADITION

Based on the Lectures
by Joshua Free

© 2022, JOSHUA FREE

ISBN : 979-8-9864379-1-0

No part of this publication may be reproduced in any form or by any means, electronic or mechanical, including photocopying, recording, or any information storage or retrieval system, without permission from the publisher. This book is not intended to substitute medical treatment or professional advice.

*The Mardukite Academy Lectures
given during September 2020
for Academy Grade-II of the
Mardukite Master Course regarding
Mesopotamian Mystery Tradition.*

Mardukite Academy Collector's Edition—*June 2022*
mardukite.com

The _Original_ Master Course Lectures

Commemorating his silver anniversary and drawing from 25 years of experiential esoteric research and underground literary developments, world-renowned mystic philosopher and prodigious occult author, Joshua Free, provides the professional qualifications necessary for "mastering" upper-level understanding of his collected works in the same way that an artist "masters" their craft. Nothing is held back in this surprisingly candid presentation of materials.

This is volume three of a four-part series, providing a serious Seeker with full transcripts to 12 of the 48 Academy Lectures previously published in the mega-anthology "Complete Mardukite Master Course."

Here you will find an insightful tome demonstrating a refreshing approach to understanding Anunnaki and Mesopotamian Traditions in the 21st century.

Although recent years have seen an advancement in the work, all publications by Joshua Free, written and published between 1995 and 2019, pertain to a singular continuum of complete instruction divided into three knowledge tiers or "Grades." A complete library collection of all "core material" described in the "Mardukite Master Course" was also reissued in four different Master Edition textbooks: "The Great Magickal Arcanum," "Merlyn's Complete Book of Druidism," "Necronomicon: The Complete Anunnaki Legacy" and "The Systemology Handbook" – totaling 3,600 pages in all.

Now YOU can experience the legendary "Master Course" from anywhere in the Universe, exactly as given in-person by Joshua Free to the "Mardukite Academy of Systemology" in September 2020.

THE GRADE-II MARDUKITE ACADEMY LECTURES

INTRODUCTIONS

Introducing the Mardukite Master Course . . . 9

Materials of the Mardukite Master Course . . . 17

Mardukite Master Course Training Schedule . . . 19

Introducing Mardukite Grade-II Materials . . . 21

THE ACADEMY LECTURES (GRADE-II)

1—25. Grade-II Introduction (*Sept. 24, 2020*) . . . 24

2—26. Mardukite Zuism (*Sept. 24, 2020*) . . . 38

3—27. The Arcane Tablets (*Sept. 24, 2020*) . . . 53

4—28. Ancient Mesopotamia (*Sept. 24, 2020*) . . . 66

5—29. Mesopotamian Magic (*Sept. 25, 2020*) . . . 79

6—30. The Sumerian Anunnaki (*Sept. 25, 2020*) . . . 93

7—31. The Anunnaki Stargates (*Sept. 25, 2020*) . . . 107

8—32. The Anunnaki Bible (*Sept. 25, 2020*) . . . 121

9—33. Necronomicon Revelations (*Sept. 28, 2020*) . . . 135

10—34. The Mardukite Core (*Sept. 28, 2020*) . . . 150

11—35. Core Review: Part-2 (*Sept. 28, 2020*) . . . 166

12—36. The Tablets of Destiny (*Sept. 28, 2020*) . . . 182

APPENDIX

Suggested Reading and Additional Materials . . . 198

INTRODUCING THE MARDUKITE MASTER COURSE

The single most purpose of our *Mardukite Master Course* is to ensure, certify and provide professional qualifications for "mastering" an understanding of the materials in the same way that an artist "masters" their craft. The complete *Mardukite Master Course* spans three *Grades* of knowledge and is given only to those *Seekers* that first properly worked through all three *Grades*, and may then be rightfully considered *Masters* of this knowledge. Extents of such "mastery" should prove readily obvious (objectively), lending to increased qualities of *Self-Actualization*, personal leadership and the certainty to manage and instruct *Mardukite Groups*.

Current works available by Joshua Free—written and published between 1995 and 2019—all pertain to a singular stream of complete instruction that is divided into three *Grades* or knowledge tiers. The *Mardukite Master Course* is intended to grant a clear unification of material presented across all three *Grades* under the banner of "Mardukite Systemology," which is also the name given to *Grade-III*. The two are interconnected (*Grade-III* and the *Master Course*); hence the complete *Mardukite Master Course* is only delivered to *Seekers* at the completion of *Grade-III*. There are "higher" *Grades* within the domain of "NexGen Systemology," but the *Mardukite Master Course* successfully covers all specifically "Mardukite Master" *Grades*: I, II and III.

It is important to clarify what we mean by *Grades* and distinguish the materials that pertain to each. In most instances, instruction for these *Grades*—as delivered in the materials (books) over the past 25 years—was all self-administered; meaning it has been explored independent of properly structured groups or trained instructors. In the past, *Seekers* selected a volume at random, had at it on their own for a while, then walked away with whatever level of understanding might be attained, even if severely fragmented. Most are unaware that the works—no matter the theme—are all tied together. They are divided as follows:

GRADE-I	Western Magical Tradition ("Magick")
GRADE-II	Ancient Mystery School of Mesopotamia
GRADE-III	Futurist/NexGen Mardukite Systemology

It can be said that the *Grades* are all a part of a single continuum—one which is explored in a "reverse engineering" style in order to provide the greatest certainty for effective workable future applications that will advance the spiritual evolution of the *Human Condition*, particularly the *Self* that is participating in and experiencing a co-creation of the Physical Universe and a continued existence of its conditions. As a single continuum, the *Grades* do actually overlap on many points—and often times these "bridges" between levels of understanding are what we are highlighting profusely for our *Mardukite Master Course*. This preferred approach—treating the universal knowledge and its records as a single wholeness rather than an emphasis on individual parts—developed after many years of experiment and discovery.

Direction of the *Mardukite Master Course* loosely follows a chronological pathway charted by Joshua Free from 1995 through 2019—meaning: from the release of the first "Merlyn Stone" *Grade-I* discourses on "magick" and "Druidism" until the recent completion of *Grade-III* as "Mardukite Systemology." Between these *Grades*, a *Seeker* discovers abundant source material known as the "Mardukite Core" comprising *Grade-II*. These *Grades* also loosely follow a premise for organization set out in the 1990's for *Grade-I* Alumni of "Merlyn Stone's School of Magick,"* that is referred to elsewhere as "The Sacred Order of the Crystal Dawn." The outline for this premise in 1999 proposed the structuring of "A New Illuminati" using the work published by Joshua Free over the next two decades.

---

* Also operating 1998-2000 as "The Elven Fellowship Circle of Magick" in Denver.

There are no strictly enforced "title-badges" and/or "initiations" defining *Grades* when applied to individual *Mardukite Groups* (outside the religious organizational function of *Mardukite Zuism* specifically) for "study" or "instructive" purposes. A *Master* may choose to adopt a particular regimen for their *Seekers* as applicable to each *Grade* and in alignment with the theme and goals of the group. Starting with the original *Grade-I* "Merlyn Stone" volume by Joshua Free—THE SORCERER'S HANDBOOK—reissued for its 21st Anniversary as a collector's edition hardcover, sufficient material is now available in each "core" toward defining group structure as it pertains to the greater "*whole*" at each *Grade*.

Parameters assigned to formal progressive *Grades* are approximately equivalent to the *first three "degrees"* of the "Crystal Dawn" program; which is the extent an individual "Chapter" or "Lodge" is allowed to administer (apart from authority of a "Grand Lodge"). For two decades, this clause permitted a *Master* of the *Third Degree* to launch a "Chapter" or "Group" as an official extension of the organization; so long as the *Seeker* had completed the *Master Course*. However, no such *Grade-III* materials were sufficiently supplied as a "core" until 2019 to make this possible.

The basic pattern of development across the *Grades* follows progressive and cumulative ascent up the "Ladder of Lights" or "Gateways to Infinity" first described by the Ancient Mystery School of Mesopotamia as a sevenfold "Babylonian Stargate" system. The chronology of the *Grades* begins with the most apparent and recent influences of the contemporary "New Age"; meaning the modern communication and conception of "magick" and metaphysics—otherwise known as the Western Magical Tradition, which maintained its popularity for the past several thousand years in Europe. This is the essence of *Grade-I*, which is essentially the "*Lunar Gate*."

A *Seeker* exploring origins behind magickal correspondences, practices, ceremonies and ritualism of various European developments—including everything from ancient Celtic Druids to more modern esoteric Hermetic Orders—will at one juncture or another intersect with the even older Ancient Mystery School present in Mesopotamia—systematized in "Mardukite Babylon" at the inception of the *Age of Aries* (c. 2160 B.C.)—an extension of the former loosely organized Sumerian civilization, now collectively making up *Grade-II* and the key to open the "*Nabu Gate*."

When a *Seeker* considers this logical progression: we begin with what is most readily familiar and accessible at *Grade-I*, loading the shot in the sling, and then pulling back to the extent that we may be certain, by examining the oldest literary records in *Grade-II*; the very basis for which our *Grade-I* material is actually based, albeit forgotten to the sands of time coupled with thousands of years of programming and encoding separating the two. History and tradition begins with "writing," and so we cannot be certain of anything further than what we have actual accounts of; yet still we find that these *Arcane Tablets* provide an understanding that is milestones beyond what is demonstrated in contemporary society today.

There are many ways of which we can demonstrate how the knowledge between these two *Grades* is bridged and overlaps in application and study; but the *Grades* are distinguished as they are for good reason—and we are not to muddy the waters of a *Seeker's* thinking by incorporating unnecessary complications to instruction. A line has been drawn, if only even from necessity, between the *Grades* by using the *Mardukite Chamberlains Grade-II* material as a benchmark for our evaluation of other materials.

Essentially—all volumes by Joshua Free pertaining exclusively to ancient Mesopotamia are considered *Grade-II*; all volumes pertaining to general mysticism, magick, esoterica, Druidism, &tc are considered *Grade-I*. This is not to say that "higher realizations" are inaccessible from lower *Grade* materials, nor is there a guarantee that "higher realizations" are gleaned directly from reading higher *Grade* materials. A *Seeker* working through the entirety of the first two *Grades* may reach all necessary "ledges" of "knowing" on their own merit, independent of outside instruction. But given that only one-way communication relay takes place from this book-learning, there is no guarantee that an individual will correctly gauge the distance between "ledges" of "knowing" on their ascent up as they leap about unaided.

An early premise of "higher" *Grades* comprised an ORIGINAL THESIS for a new flavor of "New Thought" provided exclusively to *Grade-II* Mardukite Alumni in 2011 as "NexGen Systemology." The official "Core" of *Grade-III* was not released to the public by Joshua Free until late 2019 as "Mardukite Systemology." It is from the vantage point of *Grade-III*, and a mastery of that same tier of knowledge, that we actually treat all of which the *Mardukite Master Course* represents. Although a *Seeker* could certainly remain at one or another *Grade*, an individual must demonstrate total understanding of all three *Grades* to be officially considered a *Master*.

Earliest contributions toward this *Course* from the 1990's are considered *Grade-I*, pertaining to practical magick, general metaphysics, the Western Magical Tradition and its archetypal scions, the *Druids*. The original *Grade-I* volumes pertaining to magick and metaphysics are THE SORCERER'S HANDBOOK and ARCANUM by Joshua Free. In addition to THE DRUID'S HANDBOOK, there are two volumes that both complete the *Druid Cycle* and effectively "bridge" to *Grade-II* elements that incorporate Mesopotamia: DRACONOMICON and ELVENOMICON.[*]

A *Seeker* working through the original *Grade-I* "Handbooks" may also choose to take an alternate "bridge" between the ritualism and ceremonialism of *Grade-I* with *Grade-II*, as des-

---

[*] *"Elvenomicon"* formerly released as *"Book of Elven-Faerie"* (from 2004 to 2018) by Joshua Free.

cribed in THE VAMPYRE'S HANDBOOK by Joshua Free.* The original 2015 release of these materials for *Moroii ad Vitam Paramus* served as a contemporary "holding point" for Alumni after the completion of *Grade-II* work, while a "Core" for *Grade-III* developed behind-the-scenes until late 2019. For our purposes, this now means that there are several "entry" points for a *Seeker* to experience glamour and enchantment of the *Grade-I "Lunar Gate"* on the way to higher avenues of *Self-Actualization*—which is the ultimate goal behind the *Master* level.

In 2008, existing ARCANUM and ELVENOMICON materials contributed to the establishment of *Mardukite Ministries*, an underground umbrella organization that took control of the former "Merlyn Stone" legacy of Joshua Free as a "ledge" for developing *Grade-II*. By 2009, the *Mardukite Chamberlains* emerged—a global network contributing to progressive generation and dissemination of a "Mardukite Core" of materials, providing the inception of the modern "Mardukite" (and "Mardukite Zuism") paradigms. This living spiritual philosophy dispensed at *Grade-II* is drawn heavily from the ancient cuneiform tablet records of Mesopotamia/Babylon.

Mardukite Chamberlains participated in developing the bulk of material for *Grade-II* from 2009 through 2011. These materials were simultaneously presented in two guises—the *same* materials, but dispensed in two different formats: one emphasizing the *Anunnaki Legacy* as a demonstration of more "academic" and "intellectual" pursuits into ancient history and its esoteric traditions; the other, emphasizing the title of the NECRONOMICON due to the high correlation and association of "New Age" data regarding the ancient "Mardukite Babylonian" tradition. When treated in its entirety as the *Complete Anunnaki Legacy* from within the Mardukite paradigm, presentation of the two "formats" is essentially identical. *Grade-II* should not, however, be confu-

---

* *"The Vampyre's Handbook"* formerly released as *"Vampyre Magick"* by Joshua Free; an anthology edition containing *"Vampyre Bible"* and *"Cybernomicon."*

sed with *any* other outside treatment of the "*Necronomicon*" subject.

Starting in 2009, the original source book of *Grade-II* developed into an anthology composed from individual discourses produced for the *Mardukite Chamberlains* and compiled into NECRONOMICON: THE ANUNNAKI BIBLE. Then, over the next two years, several key elements were added to expand the source book; additionally, several volumes were added to the *Grade-II* core, including Joshua Free's GATES OF THE NECRONOMICON and NECRONOMICON: THE ANUNNAKI GRIMOIRE.‡ These anthologies contain several stand-alone discourses in themselves—all of which were consolidated into a complete *Grade-II* mega-anthology titled NECRONOMICON: THE COMPLETE ANUNNAKI LEGACY (with a special *10th Anniversary Master Edition* released in early 2020).

The gradation (*Grades*) structure and concept of the *Mardukite Master Course* was announced in August 2019 at THE TABLETS OF DESTINY lectures, as described (from transcripts) in the *Grade-III* text of the same title:—

> "Some of you that have been really following along through the materials over the years already have an understanding, from the *Grades* previously provided... And this is one of the keys or secrets held by the *Master*—an individual who has a complete workable understanding of these various levels and degrees represented in former instruction, but they are not themselves formally attached to any of it—drawing up only those solid examples suitable for citation, example and demonstration. So, that's what a Master is, and we are referring now to this intermediary *Grade-III* 'Mardukite Systemology' material as the *Master*

---

‡ *"Gates of the Necronomicon"* anthology includes *"The Sumerian Legacy"* and *"Necronomicon Revelations -or- Crossing to the Abyss"*; *"Necronomicon Grimoire"* anthology includes *"The Complete Book of Marduk by Nabu"* and *"The Maqlu Ritual Book."*

> *Grade*. I expect to also develop a formal instruction course for that, which will solidify the unification of the extant 'Mardukite Core' and NexGen Systemology for this Grade."—*Joshua Free*

The other significant portion of *Grade-III* material is found within the textbook for the CRYSTAL CLEAR Mardukite Systemology Self-Defragmentation Course Program developed by Joshua Free and officially released in December 2019, so as to make certain that proper introductory tools were available for the 2020's decade to usher in a *NexGen* evolution in consciousness. *Grade-III* emphasizes strengthening personal certainty and management of "Reality," employing spiritual philosophies of "Mardukite Systemology." This is our launch point for all further upper-level *Grades*, just as much as it is a capstone representing minimum requirements for our *Mardukite Master Course*—intended to treat <u>all</u> material of *Grades I, II* and *III*.

MATERIALS OF THE
MARDUKITE MASTER COURSE

Since 2009, materials comprising the *Mardukite Research Library* have included all officially published works by Joshua Free to date. From 2008 through 2018, management and responsibility of these materials fell upon the *Mardukite Truth Seeker Press* governed by *Mardukite Ministries* and maintained by the *Mardukite Chamberlains*. As of 2018, a consistent transfer of official responsibility for all materials is increasingly assumed by the *Joshua Free Publishing Imprint*.

Throughout the years, a continuous development ensued, contributing to the release of many materials—including both those mentioned previously in this introduction, and other supplemental works that have appeared or are reissued for posterity. As the work progressed, goals for refinement and consolidation of the knowledge were repeatedly observed in newer editions and publications. Up until recently, the work was exceptionally "fluid" and required considerable attention over the course of its development. Information and discourses were released as they were discovered or refined for many years before appearing as the newly revised "collected works" anthologies and other "collector's editions" in the past year—making the materials more accessible and comprehensible than ever before possible. Goal attained.

It is of benefit for the *Seeker* (and *Master-in-Training*) to see an outright listing of all available graded materials (and their supplements) considered for inclusion as the *Mardukite Master Course*. Titles given represent the most current editions at the time of preparing this introduction. Some *Seekers* may already be in possession of former editions of these materials; and while the titles may change—and volumes may be collected for various anthologies—any "*Liber*"[*] designations used to catalogue the *Mardukite Resear-*

---

[*] The term *Liber* (meaning *book*) is used by esoteric organizations to

ch Library remain fixed to a particular discourse or release in perpetuity. This means, regardless of whatever "title" may be attached to, for example, *Liber-50* (or whatever anthology it may appear in), the material designated "*Liber-50*" is always *Liber-50*, in any of its formats or revisions. Although some *Seekers* have not taken note of these *liber designations,* this internal consistency has been maintained openly and publicly for over a decade.

MARDUKITE MASTER COURSE TRAINING SCHEDULE

|| GRADE-I || ROUTE OF MAGICK & METAPHYSICS ||

Primary Textbooks:[∞]
    THE SORCERER'S HANDBOOK
    ARCANUM: GREAT MAGICAL ARACNUM
Supplementary:
Additional: *Route of Druidism & The Dragon Legacy*

|| GRADE-I || ROUTE OF DRUIDISM & THE DRAGON LEGACY ||

Primary Textbooks:*
    THE DRUID'S HANDBOOK (*Liber-D Series*)
    ELVENOMICON (*Liber-D Series*)
    DRACONOMICON (*Liber-D Series*)
Supplementary:
    THE VAMPYRE'S HANDBOOK
    --The Vampyre's Bible (*Liber V*)
    --Cybernomicon (*Liber V2*)
Optional: *Draconomicon Vol.2: The Pheryllt Researches*
Additional: *Route of Mesopotamian Mysteries*

|| GRADE-II || ROUTE OF MESOPOTAMIAN MYSTERIES ||

Primary Textbooks:‡
    NECRONOMICON: THE ANUNNAKI BIBLE
    (-or- THE COMPLETE ANUNNAKI BIBLE)
    --Mardukite Tablet Catalogue (*Liber-N,L,G,9*)
    --The Book of Sajaha-the-Seer (*Liber-S*)
    GATES OF THE NECRONOMICON
    --Sumerian Religion (*Liber-50*)
    --Babylonian Myth & Magic (*Liber-51+E*)

∞ Grade-I, Route-A Anthology also available—*"The Great Magickal Arcanum"* (2020 Hardcover) by Joshua Free.

* Grade-I, Route-D Anthology also available—*"Merlyn's Complete Book of Druidism"* (Hardcover) by Joshua Free.

‡ Grade-II Anthology also available—*"Necronomicon: The Complete Anunnaki Legacy"* (Hardcover) by Joshua Free.

--Necronomicon Revelations (*Liber-R*)
--Crossing to the Abyss (*Liber-555*)
NECRONOMICON: ANUNNAKI GRIMOIRE
  (-or- PRACTICAL BABYLONIAN MAGIC)
--Babylonian Magic (*Liber-E*)
--The Book of Marduk by Nabu (*Liber-W*)
--The Maqlu Ritual Book (*Liber-M*)
--Enochian Magician's Handbook (*Liber-K*)
Supplementary: Optnl: *The Anunnaki Tarot* (*Liber-T*)
    Addnl: *Route of Mardukite Systemology*

|| GRADE-III || ROUTE OF MARDUKITE SYSTEMOLOGY ||

Primary Textbooks:[∞]
    THE TABLETS OF DESTINY (*Liber-One*)
    CRYSTAL CLEAR (*Liber-2B*)
Supplementary:
    SYSTEMOLOGY: ORIGINAL THESIS (*Liber-S-1X*)
    THE POWER OF ZU (*Liber-S-1Z*)
Optional: *Pantheisticon* (300th Anniversary Edition)
Additional: *Route of The Mardukite Master Course*
    Route of Professional Piloting (Grade-IV+)

[∞] Grade-III Anthology also available—*"The Systemology Handbook"* (Hardcover) by Joshua Free.

INTRODUCING MARDUKITE GRADE-II[*]

Greetings fellow Truth Seekers!

Welcome to the *Mardukite Master Course* for *Grade-II* materials!

When first starting up the *Grade-II* work, one can easily become intimidated by the multitude of books released by the *Joshua Free Publishing Imprint* (formerly *Mardukite Truth Seeker Press*). Therefore, I will here offer some advice for newcomers. All of the materials and anthologies discussed herein are also available in a single hardcover Master Edition mega-anthology titled: NECRONOMICON: THE ANUNNAKI LEGACY (2020 Edition) by Joshua Free.

The *Master Course* and/or "Chamberlain" work starts, of course, with a lot of reading. Where to begin? The question is always answered the same in *Grade-II*. Begin with our original source book: NECRONOMICON: THE ANUNNAKI BIBLE.

Approaching a mighty tome like NECRONOMICON: THE ANUNNAKI BIBLE, even in itself, might be intimidating—in fact, be aware that the current (7th) edition is a composite of at least seven individual books, each originally independently released—so here is my recommended sequence to follow for study: I suggest that you read the *Mardukite Tablet Catalogue* in the chronological order that these Tablets were first released; *not* necessarily in the "A-to-Z" order that they are arranged in that volume (which is coded as such only for the convenience of reference).

The first installment of tablets arrived in 2009 with *Liber-N*.[‡] These Tablets clearly introduce the key concepts and ideas developed throughout the book and the greater whole of

---

[*] Based on a bulletin by David Zibert originally titled *"Getting Started as a Mardukite Chamberlain"* (December 2019).

[‡] *Liber-N*, originally titled *"Necronomicon of Joshua Free"* in 2009.

the *The Anunnaki Legacy*. Yet, before even doing that, a *Seeker* is encouraged to carefully read through all introductory materials, as stated in the forewords. Take your time.

When you are ready to really dig in, read the tablets in this order: A, B, C, F, G, K, M, N and R. Once you have familiarized yourself with the first set, then proceed with remaining tablet sets as they were released in additional *Necronomicon* supplements of 2009, which proceed as *Necronomicon Liturgy & Lore (Liber L)* with the tablets D, E, L, P, T, and Z; then *Necronomicon Gatekeepers Grimoire (Liber G)* with the tablets O, X and Y; and finally *Necronomicon Shadows (Liber 9)*, consisting of tablets H, I, J and Q. This is all that constituted the very first edition of the original source book for first active year of the *Mardukite Chamberlains*.

After you are at least familiarized with the content from these tablets, it is time to set NECRONOMICON: THE ANUNNAKI BIBLE aside for a moment and do not be too concerned if you have not reached a full working knowledge of the material.

The next step is to pick up the GATES OF THE NECRONOMICON (Core Book 2) companion anthology, which provides very important keys for gaining that working understanding of the material. After reading the discourses within the anthology—*Liber 50 (Sumerian Religion)*, *Liber 51 (Babylonian Myth & Magic)* and *Liber R (Necronomicon Revelations)*—then resume with NECRONOMICON: THE ANUNNAKI BIBLE, rereading the material, including "The Book of Sajaha the Seer" (*Tablet-S*) and "The Book of Marduk by Nabu" (*Tablet-W*).

The above sequence of study provides a very solid intellectual understanding of the *Grade-II* material. All of the elements tied to its functional practice as "magick" or "religion" are tied to the *Seeker's* own background. For example, prior to any practical "Gatekeeping" it is advisable if the *Seeker* possesses a background in effective traditional magical practices.

It is assumed for the purposes of the *Mardukite Master Course* that the *Seeker* has worked through the *Grade-I Route of Magick and Metaphysics*, &tc. At this point, if you do not have any prior magickal background, you should, at the very least, read THE SORCERER'S HANDBOOK as you see fit. An additional anthology was prepared to assist personal certainty called NECRONOMICON: THE ANUNNAKI GRIMOIRE (Core Book 3), which reprints *"The Book of Marduk by Nabu"* and *"Maqlu Ritual Book"* along with additional useful applications and tips, including the texts from *Liber-E* and *Liber-K*. You might then feel ready to do some practical *Gateworking*.

The best and simplest advice when approaching the practical work is described as "three steps" in the introduction section titled: *"First Steps Toward Gatekeeping."* Stick to these and you will find the *Grade-II* work quite safe and effective.

Upon reaching a satisfactory personal certainty regarding the *Mesopotamian Mysteries*, a *Seeker* is then prepared to engage in a crossover to *Grade-III* with THE TABLETS OF DESTINY.

: LECTURE 25—GRADE-II INTRODUCTION :
(September 24, 2020)

[*Okay, this is the twenty-fifth lecture of the Mardukite Master Course; it's the first lecture of the Grade-II material. So, congratulations on making it halfway through the Mardukite Master Course. And we've already covered, in the previous half—the previous lectures—information concerning Grade-I, both routes: the Route of Magick and Mysticism; the Route of Druidism. That composes what was originally the "Merlyn School" divided into one faction that was specific to "Magic" and another faction that was specific to "Druidism." And then also, as a result of that, the Route of Druidism—we ended up developing the Route of Mesopotamia; exploring the origins of Druidism as leading into Mesopotamia.*]

So, what we are concerned with now, where the first half of the course concerned materials that are specific from the "Merlyn Stone" period in the 1990's all the way up to 2008 and the founding of the Mardukite Ministries—in 2008, I began Mardukite Ministries, which eventually changed its name in 2009 to the Mardukite Research Organization that was better known as the Mardukite Chamberlains. The work of the Mardukite Chamberlains went on for nearly a decade —actually over a decade—as it ran into the work of Mardukite Systemology, which ended up becoming Grade-III.

What we are concerned with, in regards to Grade-II material —the Route of Mesopotamia—is essentially the *staple* of what is considered the "Mardukite Tradition," the modern "Mardukite Tradition" as I established it in 2008, the Summer Solstice of 2008. And at that time, the only materials that we actually had were the Grade-I materials. And as a result of the release of "*Arcanum*," I actually was simultaneously launching the Mardukites—and this work evolved into what is now Grade-II material, which is now completely collected (in) the Master Edition; this new hardcover 2020 edition printing of "*Necronomicon: The Complete Anunnaki Legacy.*"

And this core hardcover, unlike Grade-I, all the other grades really only have one primary textbook. Grade-I is divided into the two routes with an enormous amount of research and background material as a Grade-I foundation to move upwards. And now, in Grade-II, we are dealing specifically with Mesopotamia.

Within Grade-II, we actually find the "Core Materials" that have been evolved into what we now call "Mardukite Zuism." But, for the purposes of exploring the "Mardukite Chamberlains" material, as it was researched and developed from 2008 through, really, being refined finally for this... I mean, this year—within the last couple years—at least a decade of refinements. And now with the introduction, we now use "*Mardukite Zuism: A Brief Introduction*"—the content from that—as our "Introduction" into this Grade-II material, which is actually the original publication (a small booklet publication) from when we launched, very recently, "Mardukite Zuism" as a traditional religious spiritual path that one can actually take.

Up until recently, and as we're going to treat it for this course, Mardukite work was primarily esoteric, academic and mystical; involved a lot of research; involved a lot of spiritual and other types of "technologies"; various experiments and a lot of "give and take" around the world. This was a global underground organization that launched primarily using the internet as its medium in 2008 and started building a lot of inertia and mass in 2009.

And as a result of that work, we now have this "*(Necronomicon) Complete Anunnaki Legacy*" and we've been able to solidify or "seal up" what we consider the Grade-II materials within this text. And of course, this thousand-page volume actually [*laughs*] includes the material from *fifteen* different books; many of which you may already have various previous editions of.

But they're all—for the purposes of finally making the complete and final "Necronomicon" edition—this "*Necronomicon: Complete Anunnaki Legacy*" hardcover Master Edition that we released with the "Joshua Free Imprint" for 2020, is essentially the epitome, the apex, the final result of, as I say, over a decade of developments. And these are the materials that we're going to treat for Grade-II of the Mardukite Master Course as outlined within this book; and the appendix to this book includes the material and outline for the Grade-II Mardukite Master Course, the same as which appears in your "Instructor's Manual."

So, we're going to treat this as it was explored within the Mardukite Chamberlains—in terms of Mardukite Zuism specifically, I do plan on actually releasing separate texts and separate courses for "Mardukite Ministers," things that are going to involve the religious connotations, the modern incorporation of "Mardukite Zuism" and a "Church of Mardukite Zuism" as an institution and addition to the Academy for Systemology and our Systemology Society.

All of that are practical and fundamental and futurist developments that are derived from this work—but for the purposes of the Mardukite Master Course, we're concerned with the Grade-II material as it was researched, as it was discovered, and as it can be relayed, within courses on the "Route of Mesopotamia."

Now, this may be in addition to or separate from "Wizard Schools" that you've used to bring people in, or as we do at the Mardukite Academy here, we pretty much treat all of the grades as accessible—we don't overlap them. We've... for example, I gave a previous series of lectures and education concerning specifically Grade-I; and although at a Master Level, I relayed a lot of information that overlaps the various grades, obviously I treated all that *as* Grade-I.

Now, we're dealing with Grade-II. I'm assuming that you've already been familiar with the foundations and the material that's been covered previously—and now we're dealing with the future development of that. All the work that I developed primarily between 2008 and *now*, everything not specific to Systemology, is now contained within *Necronomicon: The Complete Anunnaki Legacy.*

And what has now become *"Necronomicon: The Complete Anunnaki Legacy"*—an entire grade of materials composed into one anthology and drawing from what was previously *fifteen* different publications—actually began in the Spring of 2009. And in 2009, I was just forming what the "Mardukite Chamberlains" would be. There were no other publications yet. There was just the *Arcanum, The Book of Elven-Faerie* and *The Sorcerer's Handbook* materials at this juncture.

So I released an underground publication, which was distributed very minimally, called *"Marduk and the Anunnaki"* and that came out (for) the Spring Equinox of 2009. And so, really, the development began with this—much like the *Draconomicon*—it began with, like, a 30-page pamphlet or booklet that I just kinda distributed underground. And it was prompting the revival of interest in ancient cuneiform tablets for the basis of, what we are calling now, the "Mardukite Tradition"—and then also the use of any spiritual, mystical, magical, occult elements that might be attached to that.

That was basically where it started; and to essentially establish a "New Babylon"—a Babylonian Tradition for *present times*, and essentially doing in the 21st Century A.D. the Mardukite resurgence of the 21st Century B.C. material; and a lot of this being *prophetic*. There's a lot of prophetic—and this isn't illustrated in any of the books—but there are a lot of prophetic details; there were a lot of instructions—there was a lot of work that I was doing, starting in the 1990's, that I wasn't writing about, wasn't talking about, and really wasn't making a big thing about until I knew I had something to present.

And even though I didn't really have any publications tied specifically to it yet, if you look at the *Arcanum* material—the *Great Magickal Arcanum*—you will see elements there amidst the traditional Grade-I materials of, for example, ritual magic or spells or candle colors and things of that nature; you will see that there are other entrees within there that specifically start directing attention towards origins in Mesopotamia and then also elements of a higher unification of all these concepts, such as what we have now seen with Systemology.

So, much of that was set forth in that text; and that text—*Arcanum*—being the very first actual "Mardukite" text—the first text ever published and released by "Mardukite Truth Seeker Press"—and that was on the Summer Solstice of 2008. Now, it took another six months to even start developing an online presence. And even after that, another three months to start synthesizing the flavor and idea behind what a "Mardukite"—specifically a "neo-Mardukite Babylonian" reconstructive spiritual system that was, not *just*, for example a "Babylonian form of Wicca" or some kind of Druidry that just simply uses "Mesopotamian" concepts overlaid on it.

I was looking for the *true* work, the true knowledge, the true ancient teachings that later had been watered-down and synthesized and reevaluated time and time again over all these various cultures.

Now the *irony* behind this is that Grade-II work actually resulted as an apex into the inception of solid Grade-III material. Although Mardukite Systemology had been kind of an underground—pretty much only Alumni; those that were really high ranking within the organization. And we're not very hierarchical by the way; the thing there being that we could really only involve—given the way that this material is relayed, given the way that most people have come into our *fray*; basically interested in various aspects due to whatever their previous background was, or whatever organizations or groups they had been in—we were developing a very specific Mardukite paradigm semantic set, in terms of what is now relayed as, for example, as *The Complete Anunnaki Legacy* here in this *Necronomicon*.

And this concept of the "Necronomicon" came up almost immediately, because when I began to compose all of the materials that we're going to go into, the first real "Mardukite Chamberlains" book, which was "*Liber-N*" and originally just released as "*Necronomicon of Joshua Free*." This material—prior to even giving it that name, when I looked at what tablets we were including, the basis for the tradition, the elements that would be involved, the Anunnaki Gates, the Ladder of Lights that was going to be incorporated as a "Pathway to Ascension" and all of these elements: there was really only one aspect that, you know, that at all related or compared when it came to the modern "New Age" or even the underground "esoteric movements" and that was the "*Simon Necronomicon*."

Of course, there's other reasons why that name, you know—there's Lovecraftian and other, concerning the Cthulhu Mythos, and other reasons why "Necronomicon" is sometimes incorporated into the Anunnaki Legacy and concerning Ancient Babylon and Mesopotamia—and some of the main themes we've talked about, when we're referring to the "Dragon Legacy" and "Marduk" and "Tiamat" and all the different—the elements—involved with that.

We're talking "cosmic gateways," and different factions; we're talking about "Elder Gods" versus "Ancient Ones" and so forth. These are elements found in Lovecraftian "fantasy-horror" stories that have been, kind of, grouped together around this ancient concept that was, for all intents and purposes, mostly fabricated—yeah—by H.P. Lovecraft. But most of the themes and concepts behind it, regardless of the names that he gave to it, there's definitely elements that, for the last hundred years, many various branches—including the O.T.O., you know, the Ordo Templi Orientis and other followers of, for example, Kenneth Grant's "Typhonian" tradition and so forth.

There have been many parallels made, which is actually one of the—the subject—of one of the works within our Grade-II material, which was "*Necronomicon Revelations.*" "*Liber-R*" began to associate and correspond, for our purposes officially—because I rarely actually wrote of such topics; really in only two materials: one being "*Necronomicon Revelations*" which is contained in here, and the other being "*Liber-555*"— are really the only times I treat the outer or the modern or "Simonian" or "Lovecraftian" mythos in connection to the "Necronomicon." Otherwise, in exception to the *name*, the Anunnaki Legacy material that you're treating in Grade-II is almost exclusively pertaining to ancient Mesopotamia and not any of the "Necronomicon" or "Lovecraftian" associations attached to it.

Now there *are* individuals out there that have used our work —particularly those *Libros* that I mentioned, and then also the remainder of it—to basically form their own "Dark Societies" and "Lovecraftian Schools" and "Cthulhu Clubs" and *all kinds* of stuff like that. But that, of course, is not the actual intent of *our* work—and so really, when we're talking about the Mardukite Academy of Systemology or Grade-II, being an evolution past your "Merlyn Schools," your Wizard or "Druid Schools"—we're treating the "Route of Mesopotamia" and this is, for all intents and purposes, the *core* of "Mardukite Zuism." We're simply not exploring it as a religious premise here; we're exploring it in the same respects, for the Mardukite Master Course, as we would explore the "Druidry" and ritual magic and the "Elven Tradition" and everything that we explored in Grade-I.

It's only when an individual actually *chooses* to take this and say, "Yes, Mardukite Zuism is something that I'm going to practice as a personal spiritual path," or that they decide to get involved in "Mardukite Systemology" and higher levels of Systemology and the "Zuist" philosophies that are incorporated into *that*, that an individual might choose to take on certain—if they want to be associated as I say, with a group or a certain semantic or title or label, or however, or direct involvement with our organization.

Otherwise, we're treating it the way we've been treating it for the last over a decade, where anyone that has access to the purchase of books—that can actually buy these books— and have access to it in their own home or access to the lectures or access to *you* as the Instructor, as a mentor, administrator (if you're working in the offices) or however you're relaying this work, that we can actually teach and demonstrate this stuff as we would any other element or "Magic School" or piece of academia.

This is not specifically a study *only* for, like I said, Mardukite Zuism or so forth. And so, I already have intended to separate more of that from this so that we can actually deal a separate Course for the "Mardukite Ministers" in our Mardukite Zuist Tradition.

So, within the contents of the Grade-II textbook, there are prefaces to all of the previous editions of the "*Necronomicon*" ranging from its original release in May 2009, running through all of its various revisions into 2018. So you have, as part of the Mardukite Heritage edition that this essentially representing—because we've basically pulled in virtually all the documents, all the notes and folders, all of the materials in composing *Necronomicon: The Complete Anunnaki Legacy*.

I basically made sure that we could dig out as much of the archives as possible to get into this edition to make it as a complete as possible—to be a complete snapshot of the work of the Mardukite Chamberlains that took place for essentially a decade; and it's a pretty impressive [*laughs*] volume of material. So we have all those "Introductions" in there. I mention that again, as far as the text is concerned, the *"Mardukite Zuism: A Brief Introduction"* booklet is used to introduce all of the remainder of the text after the original "Introductions."

Then, we deal with *"Ancient Mesopotamia,"* which is *"Liber 51"* (*slash*) "52"—and that is because *"Liber-51"* was originally released as *"Babylonian Myth and Magic"* and it was later revised with a series of update pamphlets that were referred to as *"Liber-52"* once it was later integrated with the other work—and so now, that is essentially the original *"Babylonian Myth and Magic"* material; and that (text) introduces *"Liber-50,"* which was originally released as *"Sumerian Religion."*

(This all) originally became part of the *"Gates of the Necronomicon"* anthology of material—*"Liber-50"* along with *"Babylonian Myth and Magic"*—and so later, I ended up writing another piece of material called *"Babylonian Magic,"* which was meant to be connected to the "Magan Text" or "Tablets of Creation"—the *"Enuma Eliš"*—and it was originally called *"Magan Magic."* It was later retitled as *"Babylonian Magic"* when we were no longer releasing *"Liber-51"* as its own (title). But (*"Magan Magic"*) was *"Liber-E."*

And so those three texts—what's now given as: *"Ancient Mesopotamia"*; *Liber-50*, which is now given as *"The Sumerian Anunnaki"*; and *Liber-E*, which is given as *"Babylonian Magic"*—and the "Liber" designations, as you know, with the Mardukite Materials, are all that matters in terms of the designation; because the titles and the anthologies and where they appeared changed so many times over the last decade—but these "Liber" designations remained fixed; and it's for that reason that we've been able to maintain the integrity of exploring this body of material and not lose anyone along the way, in terms of how they first across it—since many of our Alumni were accessing this when it first came out under different titles.

That being said: "*Liber-51*," "*Liber-50*" and "*Liber-E*" are all given (in the Master Edition) as "introductory material" to "*Necronomicon: The Complete Anunnaki Bible*"—and "*Necronomicon: The Anunnaki Bible*" is the original Year-One material that spanned an entire catalog of tablets, which we label Tablets "A" through "Z" and these tablets were composing, essentially, what appeared to be a "Bible."

I mean of course, when we consider a "Bible" as a "book," there were no such "bound" forms of it in Ancient Mesopotamia—but what they composed was inherently the entire scriptural tradition. And so the tablet series of our "Anunnaki Bible" have actually appeared in many many editions, many revisions; it was added to, successively, over that decade of its development. It appears—from the "Joshua Free Imprint"—it appears in hardcover as "*Necronomicon: The Anunnaki Bible.*"

It also appears in paperback as simply "*The Complete Anunnaki* Bible," since many people have been often concerned about... use of "Necronomicon" in the title to represent the Mesopotamian tradition. And that's another reason I do distinguish the Mardukite Master Course, the Mardukite Materials, Mardukite Chamberlains development and this Grade-II presentation *from* "Mardukite Zuism."

In "Mardukite Zuism" *proper*, for the "Church of Mardukite Zuism," we're dealing with the exact same [*laughs*] material, in terms of ancient history—the concept or the description or descriptive title of "Necronomicon" *isn't applied*. So, in terms of "Mardukite Zuism"—because this has been a question that's come up, and I know there will be some, you know, people will invent answers over time if one's not given.

"Mardukite Zuism" is the presentation of the key elements discovered *in* the Grade-II material *of* the Mardukite Research Organization—or the Mardukite Chamberlains—which *they*, you know, *we* as the "Mardukite Chamberlains" treated as the "*Necronomicon.*"

Well—what we're doing now is developing "Mesopotamian Neopaganism" with its spiritual offset being our "Systemology," without really emphasizing the overtones of, for example, "Necronomicon" or emphasizing the "occult" overtones, for example of the "magick" and "wizardry" and "occultism," where we are actually looking at a spiritual tradition that is just drawn directly from the key elements of ancient times.

And so that being the difference between, for example, Grade-II Mardukite Mesopotamian research and development *and* what has later evolved as "Mardukite Zuism"—which evolved along with our development of "Systemology" as well. So those two, which evolved from this, are still treated as separate. In *this* instance, for *this* huge anthology and for the purposes of our Master Course where we're covering all this material... there's, you know, there's no holds barred.

So, we're looking at it as it was developed; we're looking at it as it was originally titled; we're looking at all the elements it was connected to—whether they be Lovecraftian or the Typhonian traditions, you know, all these elements—and then again, when we're treating "Mardukite Zuism," the "Church of Mardukite Zuism," the "Systemology Society" and so forth, we don't disregard all of this past text as if it didn't exist, but the emphasis is on the *key* elements at that point—and the ones that are not as fixed to *this* "esoteric" or "occult" presentation.

Now, of course, as some of you know, the materials that actually compose the "*Necronomicon: Anunnaki Bible*"—which is the main center point of our Mardukite Tradition and also *this* anthology—was, in and of itself, released in several different discourses. You had "*Liber-N*" in May of 2009, and then—which was just "*Necronomicon*"; then "*Liber-L*" came a month later as "*Necronomicon: Liturgy and Lore*"; and then

"*Liber-G*" was the "*Necronomicon Gatekeepers Grimoire.*"

Then, "*Liber-9*" was originally released as "*Nine Gates of the Kingdom of Shadows.*" "*Liber-9*" actually ended up moving into (a) domain that was later treated as "*Liber-R*," and in other works—but, in terms of the tablet material, that's where those came from. And then a few years after that, we completed translation materials for the "*Maqlu Text*" and also "*The Book of Sajaha the Seer.*"

And so all of those materials—those texts—actually appear within *Necronomicon: The Anunnaki Bible* in and of itself. And then alongside, when we released "*Liber-50*," there was also "*Liber-W*"—which is "*Complete Book of Marduk by Nabu*"—which was a series of prayers and a handbook of ritual texts and invocations that could be used in a modern Mardukite Tradition.

Of this, in Mardukite Zuism, we still have preserved "*Book of Marduk by Nabu*"—there's actually a hardcover edition, a pocket hardcover, called *The Complete Book of Marduk by Nabu* that includes all that material and actually a little bit even more than that. And then the "*Maqlu Text*" is also available in a pocket hardcover for Mardukite Zuism. So both of those elements have actually been retained for Mardukite Zuism.

[*And then, I can show you here, this is actually the new—it's the "New Standard Zuist Edition" of "The Anunnaki Bible."*] And *this* one eliminates a lot of my commentary and a lot of the superfluous information concerning what you might have as a "pocket bible" for this tradition; and it also includes "*Mardukite Zuism: A Brief Introduction*" to set it up—it's a beautiful edition *here* and these three texts: the Zuist edition of *Anunnaki Bible* and *The Complete Book of Marduk by Nabu* and *The Maqlu Ritual Book* are the three texts that have been retained for Mardukite Zuism at this juncture.

We have other materials and other work planned as we establish the "Founding Church of Mardukite Zuism" a little more properly, but these *three* have been retained—and so that is your bridge point, again we're looking for bridges sometimes when I deliver this Mardukite Master Course, so that's your bridge to that.

And then, "*Liber-R*" is included here—"*Necronomicon Revelations*"—I've talked about that a little bit, along with "*Liber-555*," which is mainly pertaining to the Simon Necronomicon and other, kind of, "modern" ritual or magical commentary concerning the various presentations of "Necronomicon" or "Babylonian Magic."

I've also included as an Appendix in here [*"Necronomicon: The Complete Anunnaki Legacy" Grade-II Master Edition*]—we released, a while back, it was mainly a combination of a few essays I had delivered to the Mardukites, and then also material drawn out of *Arcanum*; it's called "*Enochian Magic and Kabbalah.*" And the point behind this was really to try and establish that these "Anunnaki Beings" or what we treat in ancient Mesopotamia, the work involving them—the mystical work; the magical work—is more or less parallel to what we see evolving concerning this "holy divine magic"—whether it be the "Kabbalah" or the "Enochian System" and such—the same concepts behind it evolving over time, but changing based on the interpretations or the semantics of what figures these are.

So, I put forth that: whether we're talking about "aliens" or "inter-dimensional beings" or "gods" or "avatars" or "elves" or "faeries" or "angels" and "demons," that we are basically dealing with this phenomenon of the "Other" and these "beings" which, you know, are basically the backbone —whenever you look at the "ceremonial magics" and all of these things, you know, like in Grade-I, you see this stuff crop up so much that it seems like it should have some kind of parallels or origins or some kind of unification. And so, those essays are included in there. Along with that, actually, some excerpts from the *Arcanum* material for convenience factor and for reference.

And then, finally, I was able to work with Kyra Kaos—that's been doing a lot of the graphics for us, the book covers for the "Joshua Free Imprint" and the logos for Systemology—and I was able to work with her a couple years ago on completing this concept that I had had since 2009, actually, concerning the "*Anunnaki Tarot.*"

The "Joshua Free Imprint" released a small paperback book that actually had card images in the back that you could cut out and make your own set. There *was* a brief period where we actually had a limited edition physical "card set" released—and we'll probably do something similar with that again in the future. But, the material concerning the *Anunnaki Tarot* is actually also contained within this Grade-II anthology *here*.

And so, for the purposes of the Mardukite Master Course, all of the materials that you'll need and everything we'll be covering for Grade-II is within "*Necronomicon: The Complete Anunnaki Legacy.*" And there was a previous printing of this a decade ago in paperback, but this new one—this new Master Edition hardcover—we released this year, surpasses *any* of the former presentations, collecting every bit of Mardukite material and research we could possibly find, during the whole time, we were operating from different offices and releasing various books, and this... a truly indispensable resource—especially for the Mardukite Master Course.

: LECTURE 26—MARDUKITE ZUISM :
(September 24, 2020)

The materials of the Mardukite Master Course for Grade-II therefore include: all materials within *"Necronomicon: The Anunnaki Bible"*—or *"The Complete Anunnaki Bible,"* which has the Mardukite Catalogue and *"The Book of Sajaha the Seer."* We are also using materials from *"Gates of the Necronomicon,"* which has the *"Sumerian Legacy"* (which is *Liber-50, 51* and *52*) and *"Necronomicon Revelations,"* which is *Liber-R*, along with *"Crossing the Abyss,"* which is *Liber-555*. We're also using materials from the anthology *"Necronomicon: The Anunnaki Grimoire"* or *"Practical Babylonian Magic,"* which includes the *"Babylonian Magic"* essay from *Liber-E*, *"The Book of Marduk by Nabu"* materials, *"The Maqlu Ritual Book"* and, of course, *"Enochian Magic and Kabbalah."*

All of these materials are contained within the Grade-II textbook for the Mardukite Master Course, which is *"Necronomicon: The Complete Anunnaki Legacy."* However, many individuals will have already had access to some of this, previous from these separate editions. And all of this material we are basically going to be covering for Grade-II.

So, this whole body of material—for over a decade now—has been referred to as the "Mardukite Core." And that meant the "Mardukite Core" *body* or Core *basis* of material being essentially literary.

What we have always been concerned with, in regards to following a tradition—a literary, a written, a recorded tradition—throughout thousand of year, has been specifically *these* records, these *written* records; without them, we don't really have "history"—what we have is "archaeology." We have digging up "pots" and trying to determine dates based on layers of soot over them and so on and so forth. But nothing concrete; nothing to really make a basis of understanding from. And so what we've done is basically traced back the written records.

In Grade-I, we're going back at least as a far as to 2,500 years ago—but when we're dealing with Grade-II, we're going back *6,000 years* of written recorded "history" and "knowledge" (and) "beliefs" (and) traditions and such. And this is about as far as we can go back—not that this is the *origin* of everything, and that's something that we have to point out, you know, here at the beginning.

Because we *do* refer to "Mesopotamia" as the "Cradle of Civilization," but what we mean is the "cradle" of *our* current conception of Human civilization. We don't mean that it's the origins of everything that *ever* was and has been and that nothing came before. We actually know that that's false. We know that this is probably been happening on Earth for a very very very long time—and that we've simply just cycled through another manifestation of it; another demonstration of a systematized society.

And so what we're dealing with, is we're dealing with what we can actually "know" at a literary level—I mean, there's obviously other "spiritual" ways of working with knowledge and other aspects, which we actually deal with at, you know, "upper levels" of Systemology, but for Grade-II purposes, we're still dealing with an "academic" tradition; we're still... Grade-I and Grade-II are academic traditions, which can be relayed very easily as "courses" that are tied into either "fields of study" that are very, you know, very familiar to those working with these things or watching various programs on T.V. or on the internet and can be tied into the "academics" such as you would study at a "school." When we get to "Systemology," we're dealing with just "advanced," you know, the "Next Level" of such things.

For our intents and purposes though, Grade-I and Grade-II are dealing with "records." We're dealing with *6,000* years of

Human history; we're dealing with the "origins" and "inception" of *systems* of *this*—as we understand Human civilization today—because most of these... most of what we understand today—most of what we take for granted, most of what has been going on around us—these are all part of this "cog-wheel" systematic process of the way these different facets and such of the "wholeness factor" have been relayed in Human understanding all throughout thousands of years.

These are evolutions are further developments and refinements of the exact same systems that we find developed in Mesopotamia. And... *Oh,* everything from the idea of "real estate," the idea of, you know, "property lines," "boundary markers" for property lines; the use of "paved roads" and even the idea of needing specific "roads" and developing stuff that would be on them, such as like the "chariots" and things of that nature. This all became conceived of at the time. The idea of "schooling systems," idea of "taxation"—most of the structure of "governments"; everything that we know concerning the fundamental structure of "monarchies" and "priesthoods," the development of "kingdoms" and all of the infrastructure attached to that—that was all conceived of first in Mesopotamia, in regards to the civilization, that *we* understand it as, for the last *6,000* years.

Now, this information spread; and this information was *given.* It was *spread* to others; it was *given* from "higher minds" and "higher minds" that were probably involved with the, you know, the "fallings" of the "previous" ones—or were able to care-take knowledge of the previous *age,* the previous civilization, for which we really don't have any written records. And that's why we draw our line with Mesopotamia, in terms of our academics—or our studies—or our esoteric archaeology.

Because what we're concerned with are written records. And although civilizations may have indeed come before us, we just don't simply have enough records of them—even if they leave behind *even more* ancient, like the bases underneath structures, certain ruins, other feats of great engineering that may still remain... none of it really gives us enough to base "traditions" of knowledge off of. We're not dismissing that these things exist, we're just saying, "well, history begins with writing" as far as we're concerned. Everything else is "prehistory"—"prehistoric." We don't dismiss that the dinosaurs exist either, but we're dealing with the records as we, you know, pertain to the last 6,000 years...

In *that* example, one of the crossovers would be, for example, the *Sirrush Dragon*: the "Dragon of Babylon," essentially the "royal pet" of the Mardukite family lineage. And you see this image on the walls... we talked a bit about it when we're discussing the "Dragon Legacy" in Grade-I. And the records of this would really indicate that it may have been left over from the dinosaur age—that this was simply a very rare being that was considered a "dragon." But the descriptions of it are not so unrealistic to, you know, other creatures that we've found evidence for in the past.

Now although Mardukite Zuism is considered, essentially now, a separate aspect of our presentation of material—we're now treating Mardukite Zuism as the practical faction, or the practical evolution, of what the Mardukite Chamberlains and the Council of Nabu and such for the Mardukite Organization, once was. Since we've now capped off our "Core" of material for Grade-II and released this anthology and are able to deliver it as a "Master Level" course, we've actually *evolved that* organization now.

So, the Mardukite Chamberlains became basically the basis of two further developments: one of which being Mardukite Zuism; the other being the Systemology Society. And so those are two evolutions that actually spawn from the Grade-II work that we're going to be studying more academically.

Now, of course, as Mardukite Academy of Systemology, we're delivering "courses" and being that we're doing this from, for example, the Offices and the Founding Church of Mardukite Zuism—and the development of our Systemology Society—of course, that's what we would be inclined to want to encourage those to be... to get involved with and be a participant with what we're growing with this.

However, for the purposes of the Mardukite Master Course, we're mainly treating it as a study, like we would with the Druid School or the Wizard School, that we're treating it as it was treated by the Mardukite Chamberlains—which weren't just doing so passively.

The Mardukite Chamberlains were very serious about the development of this work and how important it was to get it out there and to relay this as, kind of, a "fundamental" of the backbone of "history." Like the stuff that really wasn't being dealt with.

Now we do see a little bit more of a treatment of it—for example, on various television shows—but, at the time [with the Mardukite Chamberlains] this is, kind of, being developed up from scratch; and we were doing a lot of "trial and error," a lot of revisions, a lot of new presentations—trying to get it *down* to a point where we could actually have something solid that we could then integrate as a modern tradition.

That being the case—there really is no other, for example, "Mesopotamian Neopaganism" or true "Babylonian Mardukite Reconstructionism" in any way, shape or form. Now, we are not doing the exact same stuff that they were doing back then. It simply wouldn't be relevant to do that. We can still study the history, be inspired by it, figure out the common points and the themes, but our reenactment of it, for example, in Mardukite Zuism and such, is really a bridge to higher levels of understanding.

The point of it though is that it's a solid "*ism*." We have something now that we can actually have, you know, gather under—which was really important. Because it's been very loosely organized up until now. And so by calling it "*Mardukite Zuism*," those that have been involved for so long, now have something to, kind of like, sink their teeth in as like: "This is what I am"; "This is what I've been doing"; "I've been working at this for over a decade, now, and been a part of its development and..." you know, what is *it*? What do I call *this*? What is *this* philosophy?

Especially with the integration of the new Grades of Systemology, we established a new—like a *new* "evolution" of the Mardukite Tradition as a bridge to that; and that became "*Mardukite Zuism.*"

Now, in Sumerian, the word "ZU" means "to know" or "knowingness." And of course, we know that in the Babylonian Mardukite Tradition and its refinement of Akkadian into essentially its own Babylonian language, the preservation of Sumerian words as they were given was often retained for "high spiritual" or "Divine" concepts that could then be given more esoteric meaning.

For example, "to know"—kind of like the way we would consider "*Latin*" or "*Welsh*" or any of these other languages that we've... or "*Enochian*" and so forth, "*Hebrew*"... They're considered "mystical" or "different" that, you know, certain "knowledge" or "information" or "key words" might be retained in former language.

So, even as Mardukite Babylonians, there's really no discrepancy in including some of these simple basic "*signs*" and "*logograms*" and essentially "words" of Sumerian language into the Babylonian Tradition.

And so, in our purposes, "ZU" is applied to mean not just "to know," but the *Awareness*, the *consciousness*, the "*Spiritual Life*" or "*Awareness of the Alpha Spirit*" that operates *outside* of *this* existence, that *is* the *actual* "I-AM," the *actual* "Knowingness" of Self as being Aware as a Spirit. And this goes far and beyond anything from like Descartes "I think therefore I am"—this is the One that is *doing* the Thinking and Knowing.

So, we came up with this concept from that and one of the reasons I want this up now—because it's not related in any of your books; and it is something that is going to be, you know, come up under discussion—or especially with those... We live in the internet age. So the idea of looking into other applications of this *term*... It requires me to give some background... Mainly because this idea behind "Zuism" has been used otherwise elsewhere—and so, kind of like anything else: Druidry, Christianity, any other factions of religion, you have different takes, I guess, on it. So...

When one investigates "Zuism," because this is actually... being that the Systemology Society was developing this underground, we weren't really integrating it yet until last year in 2019. And prior to this, this idea of "Zuism" for a quasi-Mesopotamian Tradition, apparently had been being used in Iceland for purposes of, basically of just incorporating a new religion for whatever the purposes are with that.

There's a lot of controversy when you look online concerning, basically, it being used as some kind of "tax shelter" or really having no significant literature or religious activities and so forth—and, I mean, *we've* already surpassed that even with the *materials* and the *work* and founding of various stuff that *we've done*. But, in having a Seeker, you know, having access to *all this information* out there on the web—they may do some investigating, look up "Zuism" and find out that it's really connected to some, like I said, some Icelandic collapsed religious attempt or so forth.

And so the idea, I guess then, behind "Zuism"—although our philosophy is unique to us—the idea behind "Zuism" in general, as a revival concept of that, is not unique to our work. However, our "Mardukite" brand of it *is*. So, "Mardukite Zuism" and virtually anything related to "Mardukite"—

which is the same reason we incorporated it in Grade-III for "Systemology." "Systemology" being first introduced as "Mardukite Systemology" in order to differentiate it from anything else.

So, the "Mardukite Core" that we are studying at Grade-II *is* the actual foundation, again, just as Grade-I was the foundation to develop a Grade-II, our Grade-II "Mardukite Core" is the foundation on which "Mardukite Zuism" *and* "Mardukite Systemology" have developed. And those are the two current *active* "evolutions" from the Grade-II work.

Obviously we're still working at the actual incorporation of various aspects of the organization and the kind of materials that are going to be specific to that—traditions, rites and ceremonies of a modern religion, aspects of clergy and such —but none of that is really specific to what you're studying at Grade-II, so it's not... although it's not ready yet, the reason that we're doing this as the Mardukite Master Course, is the whole "Mardukite Core," all of the ancient research, all of the cuneiform tablets, all of the comparative studies with other traditions and mystical systems and so forth, has already been completed.

Everything from here on out is a development of the organization as a modern organization and its structure and its modern tradition and also the evolution of its spiritual advisement and counseling services in the form of Systemology. Both of those are still ongoing developments. But they both reached outside of what we're going to treat as the Mardukite Master Course.

My intention isn't to stomp on all these other efforts or anything else that's going on out there, it's just important—if you're gonna be dealing with the Mardukite Tradition and what's being now represented as "Mardukite Zuism," or even "Mardukite Systemology," it's important to know what you're representing in your classes; and with your Seekers and when you're doing your various work. Although we're treating them separately, these are the overlapping points of it.

Another facet that had occurred prior to the incorporation of Systemology and Zuism—but of which still is pretty much treated as an underground—is a group of Alumni got together about five years ago and we were working on what is called "*Moroii ad Vitam*," which is essentially incorporating a combination of the Mesopotamian and Druidic and Systemological and so forth—concepts—into the themes of the "Vampyre" Tradition. And *that* material is available.

We have "*The Vampyre's Handbook*"—that's the hardcover 2020 edition that includes both "*The Vampyre Bible*" and "*Cybernomicon*" material. And that's *another* facet that, again, although we're not treating it directly *in* the Mardukite Master Course, it *is* basically kind of a summary using "vampyre" and various "darksider" themes in the relay of the same traditions—just an analysis of that same current that's also been operating in the underground, and of which is often the more commonly revived elements of Mesopotamia.

When you see "Mesopotamian Magick" or "Babylonian Magick" or "Sumerian Magick"—when you go and see what the *others* are doing out there; other traditions or other authors *outside* of the Mardukites and Mardukite Zuism, you'll see that most of it is primarily "dark-sided" stuff—"left-hand path" stuff—dealing with the demonology and really trying to just apply, for example, like *Keys of Solomon*, *Goetic* type—like I was saying in Grade-I: applying the same "Grade-I"-type understanding—type knowledge—to what *we* are treating here as Grade-II; because it's actually the evolution *of*—the origins *of*—when treated directly, Self-Honestly, as it actually is.

If you're gonna go into it, just applying all these other Grade-I facets to it, and trying to make it fit *that*, well then you end up with pretty much all the other authors and groups [*laughs*] have been doing for the last decade; because they have taken notice of us, but their methods and their delivery: it's still just kinda catering to that lowest level denominator in that—it's never pierced the veil of what we're treating at Grade-II.

Now, unlike former presentations, for example, the hardcover "*Necronomicon: The Anunnaki Bible,*" the pocket edition paperback of that same edition, and then "*The Complete Anunnaki Bible*" that we released about a year ago—those actually retail more of like, basically the way the Mardukite Chamberlains studied the "Bible" directly, whereas the "new versions," we are actually introducing both "*The Complete Anunnaki Legacy*" anthology and the "New Standard Zuist Edition" of "*The Anunnaki Bible*" with the text of "*Mardukite Zuism: A Brief Introduction.*"

And now that *that* is actually included *in* your textbook for Grade-II—just the "*Brief Introduction*" material for it—is at least integrated now [*laughs*] into the Mardukite Master Course and as a bridge, if one is interested in, you know, pursuing this type of work further under that premise.

The other thing that this actually does is, because "Mardukite Zuism" and "Systemology" kinda became this *new* evolution of the work, in the "*Brief Introduction*" material, we are actually introducing a Seeker, for the first time, with the Standard Model. The Standard Model is explored deeper once we get into, for example, "*The Tablets of Destiny*" material of Grade-III.

This is the first time, in terms of Grade-II material, in terms of an "*Anunnaki Bible*" or our "*Complete Anunnaki Legacy*" edition, that the material is actually being set up with this essay called "*Mardukite Zuism: A Brief Introduction.*" So, it's important that you're at least familiar with that, because that is actually the newest edition and latest improvement or "light shined" on what all of this ancient research and a decade spent in digging up old writings has basically culminated into.

Another good of point of distinction in the relay of the material—because we did a lot of research and development in terms of even just the presentation of our materials over the course of a decade—is that the Mardukite Master Course has more of a tendency, when it comes to the instructors, the Academy, esoteric schools, what we're kind of here dealing with—we've already dealt with a lot of "magick" and "mysticism" and the "enchantment" of the Druid Tradition and so forth, so what we're dealing with, when we're dealing with "*Necronomicon: The Complete Anunnaki Legacy*," we're still, kind of, in the realm of the "esoteric."

And we, kind of, maintain that for the Mardukite Master Course—because there are a lot of initiates, a lot of individuals out there, a lot of those with past experience in various schools and such of this nature; that this is their way of actually accessing this—this is their entry points into getting into the higher, for example, "Mardukite Zuism" as a spiritual tradition and the Tech involved behind "Mardukite Systemology" and the "Systemology Society." Some of that seems a little bit far reaching, or fluffy, or even too "esoteric" for those that are otherwise [*laughs*] "esoteric."

So, in developing "Mardukite Zuism" and the "*Anunnaki Bible*" for that and a tradition for that, versus what we've been, kind of, putting together (over) the last decade in the "Mardukite Core," is that we have—for those that are interested in more of that mystical side of things; those type of themes; the concept of the *Necronomicon* and that way or "route" *to* the information or to the higher gates of realization—we offer that; we offer that now within the materials we present and then also *you* being able to gauge the *cues* of the Seekers that you're working with in how to best deliver information.

And then we've just received as many responses that basically just the idea of *Necronomicon* or the idea of the *occult* or *mysticism* verbatim and those presentations are basically—have kept (some) people away. And so we've presented other alternatives, such as "Mardukite Zuism" and even our —"*The Complete Anunnaki Bible*" without *Necronomicon* in the title; it simply brings a different segment in and provides an entry point for others that might otherwise be turned off by, you know, like I say, the name "Necronomicon" or anything that *that* has attached to it.

Now, eventually we want to see an individual *able* to push *past* the filters and semantic paradigm sets and all of that, which is limiting their ability to just see all of this as it is and not suddenly have *all* these reactive associative mechanisms go off when they, for example, see the word "*Necronomicon.*"

But for purposes of the Mardukite Master Course—for the purposes of trying to reach as many individuals as we can and bring to them to these higher points of realization—we have to make sure that we have both methods.

And so that—as a Master Level instructor, given that "Mardukite Zuism" does fall within the domain at an academic and intellectual level, as the materials that you're gonna be working with for Grade-II, it's just important that we explore this; because you *will* run into this *in* your personal experiences in delivering this work—whether it's one or the other of those extremes. It will come up, so it's just one of those things that I want you to be prepared for. [*Laughs*]

Since it's introduced in the new textbooks, I figure that the "*Mardukite Zuism (Brief) Introduction*" is a good place to start; because it *does* introduce a lot of key ideas and a lot of key concepts that later come up in whatever methods, or however far, an individual is exploring the work.

So, first of all, according to the most ancient historical records—and these would be the "King Lists" and these tablets are listed as the "Tablet-K Series" within our "Mardukite

Tablet Catalogue" of materials—within the textbook. The Anunnaki begin to emerge 432,000 years ago; and that's by one count. We're actually gonna be delving into more research into the chronology of the prehistoric "King Lists," because some believe that it may be closer to 244,000 years ago.

But in either case: *hundreds of thousands* of years ago [*laughs*] these figures that we are referring to as "Self-Actualized Spiritual Beings"... Now, you know, if you want to get into different semantics of it, each one is almost its own pursuit; whether they are light beings, inter-dimensional beings; beings from the "Magical Universe," beings from a previous jump-start of civilization, as far as their encounters with the Sumerians—the tablets record that they have been here for hundreds of thousands of years.

Now, we only have 6,000 years of Human records concerning what's actually been recorded by those hands in the Ancient Near East. But according to the "King Lists," which extend leading up to those which are observed as the "kingship" *in* Mesopotamia, they're treated as having exceptionally long lifespans—and this changes at one point, when the Anunnaki actually end up getting involved with the genetics of the Human Condition—the Human genetic vehicle. They begin to limit its lifespan.

These beings are actually very very *old* presences—and as far as we can tell, they're essentially the same as the "Divine Pantheon" that appears in the Celestial Mythologies of just about all ancient history.

In Mesopotamia, we're dealing with *cuneiform*. And *cuneiform* is the oldest known writing system that we actually have any evidence for now. And we're not talking about "cave drawings" or ones that are open to, you know, symbolic forms of communication, which had existed for thousands of years prior to that—but an actual systematized system of language that was used to *codify* the—not only the verbal speech but *written records* that could be communicated and duplicated and carried across time or distances.

This *cuneiform* is used—it's made, the characters are made, with a "reed pen" or "stylus." And, for this wedge-shaped pattern that the strokes and notches of each of these, which make up these symbols; that's what gives it—from the Latin *cunei*—it gives a wedge-shape appearance and therefore the name *cuneiform*. That's where we get the word *cuneiform*.

And so, this basic (brief) introduction to Zuism, we're introducing a Seeker to just some basic terminology before going into the work; such as the concept of the "cuneiform writing," which isn't done on paper, it's done on "clay tablets." And the most ancient cuneiform writings are dealing with the descent of "King Lists" as far as the lineage and the Divine Right to Rule is passed down through these lineages from these ancient beings called the "Anunnaki," which are considered—from a religious perspective—the "gods" and "goddesses" of the "pantheon."

And this same—they're given planetary associations as well—and we'll go through all of who and what the Anunnaki are. But, they're given these basic classifications and we see, kind of, a duplication and repeat of these basic themes throughout all these later (more recent) cultures; each one of them "ancient" in their own right, but when we look at the themes and we look at the time-line, we see that when we go back to ancient Mesopotamia, there's definitely origins for most of these concepts there.

In Systemology and in Mardukite Zuism, we're dealing with the *epitome* of the Grade-II work; we're dealing with, pretty much, the "icing on the cake," the "cream of the crop"—we're "cherry picking" the best tablets, the highest understanding of the spirituality, the ways in which we can apply it now in Systemology; in a framework that has never before been conceived of, both in recorded mystical history or archaeology, and are basically taking this stuff to the next level.

[*Throughout the rest of the day and for the next couple days*] as we go through Grade-II, we'll be touching many elements that are actually approaching Grade-III as well, concerning the material being treated as "Arcane Tablets." Wherever the cuneiform tablets appear in Systemology or in Mardukite Zuism in relation to the spiritual tradition, they are referred to as the "Arcane Tablets."

And so there's a complete collection of our "Arcane Tablets" in "*The Complete Anunnaki Legacy*" (this Master Edition for the Grade-II Mardukite Master Course) and also in any of the former editions of either "*Necronomicon: The Anunnaki Bible*" or "*The Complete Anunnaki Bible*" and that composes the "Tablet Catalogue," which is the main *corpus* of the "Mardukite Core."

: LECTURE 27—THE ARCANE TABLETS :
(September 24, 2020)

Mardukite Zuism is used to introduce Grade-II because it is the future evolution of Mardukite methodology—the Mardukite Tradition that the Chamberlains spent a decade developing. And it does present many key concepts. [*Before the break*] I just brought up the Anunnaki a bit, the "King Lists," the "Arcane Tablets"—and on the Arcane Tablets there's also a mention of the legendary "Tablets of Destiny." These are, of course, the representations of Divine Truth, Supreme Knowledge, Cosmic Power of the "gods"—all of this being introduced into the cuneiform literature, the scriptural texts, in the "Epic of Creation"—the *"Enuma Eliš"*—which is, pretty much, the backbone of the Mardukite Tradition—the concept of "Marduk" as the central figure, the key Anunnaki God and patron of Babylon and Babylonian Tradition.

The "Epic of Creation" as we know it from Mesopotamia is drawn from seven cuneiform tablets. They are named the *Enuma Eliš* because of their opening lines. It's been established by most biblical scholars and those that study the Judeo-Christian tradition, the *Genesis* or even the concept of the "Seven Days of Creation" is closely paralleled to this ancient Mesopotamian lore.

So we see many parallels—academically, historically, spiritually—when we're dealing with the "Mardukite Core," because we're dealing with the Ancient Near East; we're also dealing with encounters between the Mesopotamians and the Egyptians and we're dealing with a geography which had everything to do with the establishment of the Semitic systems *including* the "Jewish Tradition," the "Kabbalah," all of which was later developed from this region—this area—and during this time. And Mesopotamia is found to be a specific origin for that.

And so, as I mentioned (*in the previous lecture*), a very basic form of the Standard Model that's now used in Systemology is given in not only the beginning of "*The Anunnaki Bible: New Standard Zuist Edition,*" but for the purposes of this Master Course, it is given at the beginning of the Grade-II textbook, "*Necronomicon: The Complete Anunnaki Legacy.*"

Although we don't spend a lot of time in Grade-II analyzing what it ends up being the subject of—"*The Tablets of Destiny*"—which is the main... the first book, which mainly prompted Grade-III to come into existence. But the origins and the seeds of that information are *here.*

And so, in the Standard Model, you see these "concentric rings" and it essentially shows the "All"—or "AN-KI"—which envelops both "spiritual existence" (AN) and "physical existence" (KI). So, we see the "ALL"—the "All of Existence"—being basically composed of the "spiritual" and the "physical" in the Model; the "physical" being the "smaller circle" in that.

"AN-KI"—which is the Sumerian word for the "All" or the "All-Universes" and "All-Existences"—is simply a composite of the two words, "AN" and "KI"; being that all "spiritual existences" and all "physical existences" *combined* form the ALL. And this ALL is divided by what is considered "Cosmic Law." And this "Cosmic Law" in some texts is referred to, for example, as the "Tablets of Destiny."

There are others that refer to the Divine "ME"—"M" "E"—these Divine "ME" or "discs" or "decrees"; there's different archaic explanations for what they might be—and we of course, explore that too at Grade-III. But this "Cosmic Law" is in place and that there is a connection—the "Cosmic Law" basically divides "spiritual" and "physical" existences. In the *Enuma Eliš*, we refer to that as the "Dragon's Head" versus the "Dragon's Body," which is separated as a metaphor for the division of Universes—separating the "physical" from the "spiritual" or even the "Land" from the "Sky" in some interpretations.

On our Standard Model, there's a line that goes through that connects All Existences; there's only one point of connectivity that connects All Existences, and we call that "Life Awareness" or "ZU" and in Systemology we refer to that as the "ZU-line"; and that has other implications concerning, for example, the fragmentation of the Spirit and its consideration of lower and lower points of Beingness as an "Identity."

But for purposes of "Mardukite Zuism" or in Grade-II exploration of the Mardukite Core, it's simply that—essentially, the point of Life Awareness and Spiritual Beingness, the Self, is the only point of connectivity between these two existences. And then, outside of all this—the outer point of this model—outside of which is the Infinity, or the "AB-ZU," which is described as an "Infinity of Nothingness" or an "Abyss."

The "Infinity of Nothingness" or the "AB-ZU" or the "Abyss" is encompassing *All* that is beyond this greater circle, which is the ALL—the Potential Everythingness—which is a spiritual existence that is confined by the "Law" and separated into a (lower) physical "Beta" existence as the "Physical Universe."

And that is about the extent that we get into the Systemology of the Mardukite Tradition. Everything else that is treated at a Grade-II level in exploring what is later considered the "Arcane Tablets" is primarily treated at an esoteric—or from the magician's perspective, or from the fact that we've just elevated out of the veil of Grade-I and we're looking at a tradition, a mythology, a pantheon, a system of priests and priestesses and an esoteric tradition and the organization of a society; but we're looking at an *archetype*—we're looking at the first one in which these others, that we have kind of tapped on in Grade-I, were based upon.

So, the reason this exploration is pretty useful is because really the backbone behind the Mardukite Babylonian Tradition, Babylonian Mythology, a lot of what we know concerning Marduk and the Anunnaki, is based on the *Enuma Eliš*, which was used as essentially the main scriptural "*Bible*" or "*Genesis*" for the "Mardukite Paradigm" in Babylon. And so, when we introduce—using the section "*Mardukite Zuism: A Brief Introduction*"—when we introduce the Seeker to the "Mardukite Core" this way, we're basically only just scraping the surface of some of the newer more recent Grade-III standards.

But what we're doing is introducing this so that the Systemology that's inherent in, at the very least, the *Enuma Eliš*, is illuminated as an individual is entering into this exploration. In doing so, as opposed to our former presentations prior to the Mardukite Master Course, it was still pretty much treated as just this "ancient study," of which was only loosely organized, and of which took, like I say, about a decade to really put together as a coherent library of material—and now, which is now contained within this one anthology.

The definitions for that basic standard of "model" for exploring "Mardukite Paradigm," "Mardukite Zuism" and "Systemology" paradigm, is given in that introductory section. And this exploration allows one to go into this study; for example, knowing about the absolute existence behind the ALL—which, you know, as is referred to on the "Tablets of Destiny" as the "Infinity of Nothingness."

Because in the past, you know, the "Abyss" is very obscurely understood. In our *new* Systemology, you understand this "Infinity of Nothingness" being contrasted with a "Potential Everythingness." And it's the "Nothingness" being the true constant *static* of just entirely unmanifest latent potential, of which is entirely manifest as a reflection or as a balance as the "Everythingness" of the "ALL."

And then we see this in the *Enuma Eliš*, this division where the "Law" or "Cosmic Law" is identified as the "Cosmic Dragon" or Tiamat. And (for) purposes of, for example, Hermetic philosophy, or a better higher understanding of the mysticism—which is basically what prompted the *New Thought* explorations attached to this that developed into Systemology—the presence of Tiamat, rather than the Nothingness, the presence of Tiamat *as* a "Creative Force," the original primordial force in the "All," *is* what we consider as the "First Cause" or the movement across a "Sea of Infinity."

So, in many respects, "she's" actually kind of, well, treated as a "feminine water dragon" that is basically creating the first tides or the first motions or the first movement across what was the "Seas of Infinity" (of Nothingness)—just the "Infinity of Nothingness," only potential, but completely unmanifest and latent energies. And so this is what is identified in the *Enuma Eliš*.

She is essentially the representation of the "Law" then; because she becomes the division between this "spiritual existence" and this "physical existence"—the defining aspect in the ALL, which permeates All Things and is almost like the "Governor" for the manifestation, almost near-infinite manifestation of that which was unmanifest.

Within *"The Tablets of Destiny"* material of Grade-III we get into this much deeper, but these were all derived from a careful exploration and study of the "Arcane Tablets" as they appeared in the Grade-II "Mardukite Core." And so, by having these, kind of, hints presented as an introduction, when an individual or Seeker or when you go back through and look at this material, it will have just a little bit more color and a little bit greater comprehension attached to it; as opposed to the more "mythological" or "fanciful" or "literal" way in which it was demonstrated.

Although a very amazing presentation of language, you know, being among the first of the cuneiform languages—we're still always dealing with what is open to interpretation; what these words and concepts actually were trying to represent, and if that message is being perfectly duplicated or not. The last one-hundred and fifty years of contemporary or traditional archaeology demonstrates that the greater understandings have *not* been understood outside of the Mardukite Research Organization and the development of Systemology and such.

So, in the *Enuma Eliš* we're presented with, basically, the "cosmological origins"; I mean, the title of the work and its first lines are referring to "when before the Heavens and Earth are named." We're talking about the formation and interaction of active existences and we talk about, in Grade-III, these systems of manifestation: Substance, Motion and Awareness—and that when you examine the "*Tablets of Destiny*" or as they're explored as the *Enuma Eliš*, you see Tiamat basically responsible for the, as I say, the governing of "substances" and "bodies," the "Life" and the "gods."

They're described as—when the Anunnaki begin coming forth—they're described as being "turbulent waves" that have "action" that carry through "space." And as the governing "faction" of "Cosmic Law," Tiamat responds accordingly; and she "fixes the Tablets of Destiny," which is the representation of Authority in the Cosmos, "to her deputy," this messenger "wave-action" of the "Law" which is named Kingu. And then that's sent rippling out to meet the Anunnaki gods.

So, what we have described is an "energetic"—almost "battle"—between formations. Some have even used this to describe the formation of "solar systems"—the formation of planets. Others have used this to describe some of what is even given in the Eastern traditions, in like the *Veda* accounts, or the idea of "battles" that we taking place in the "heavens." And it's very possible that these concepts and stories actually have a *manifold* application—that this basic concept, the basic systemology of what's described here, is not specific even to any *one* specific aspect, because it's just —it applies to *all* Systems. It's almost like the original concept of Systemology.

And so, it's in the *Enuma Eliš*—the "Epic of Creation"—that we encounter the Anunnaki and these beings prior to, again, prior to the formation of "Heaven" and "Earth" being divided or "named." And so, even in Systemology, we start to look at—we look at "alternate universes," the "division of universes," and even how they've been compartmented, fragmented, condensed; and we see, again, we see more similarities between this basic "systemological knowledge" and what takes place all throughout existence.

In the *Enuma Eliš*—in the standard version, of course—the Anunnaki Assembly of Gods are preparing to battle the Law and none of them are, basically, willing to go out and meet this wave-action—go out and actually "confront" Tiamat. And so, this is when we're introduced, for the purposes of Babylonian cuneiform texts, because that's what primarily the Mardukite tradition is based on—and you can see this wherever "Marduk" is given a centralized position.

A lot of times, a lot of the concepts between what is "Sumerian" and what is "Babylonian" is blurred; and this is something that is not—we don't have any misunderstandings about in the Mardukite Tradition, because we know that anything that observes "Marduk" in the tradition is Babylonian; and wherever, for example, Enlil or the "Enlilite" systems are treated—such as Ninurta, Ishtar, and so forth, as primary; the Sumerian Cult of the Moon, that predated Babylon, with an emphasis on Nanna, and such—we'll get into the identities of these figures later (most of you are familiar with them just from your studies already).

But such figures were specific to the Sumerian pantheon, the Sumerian worldview, to the Enlilite Order of understanding, which was very loosely ordered, loosely organized, not really systematized for the purposes of a standard tradition, and so it was really—when it was kind of usurped, taken over, by the Mardukite standard—it was easy to *do*, because a lot of the "systems" weren't already in place; a lot of the pantheistic understandings, the system of religion, the idea of standardizing a whole methodology, this was actually all *new*, even though it was using Anunnaki figures from the prior Sumerian age.

One of the "giveaways"—when we look at the *Enuma Eliš*, because sometimes this has been referred to as the "Sumerian Genesis" or the "Sumerian Origins" rather than Babylonian—is the fact that Marduk volunteers to be the hero that confronts Kingu and Tiamat. And this is one of his—the first mentions of that name in cuneiform literature.

Prior to this, Marduk is not really given a position in the Sumerian pantheon. And so, the Mardukite lineage—which puts more of an emphasis as Enki as Master of the Magicians and then later Marduk as Master of the Magicians, with Nabu as High Priest; and Nabu then, basically, charged with the tradition and the "magic" of the prior age—we're dealing with a completely different lineage than what was set down in the original "Sumerian" concept and worldview under Enlilite Ordering; we're dealing with a "New World Order" of Enki, we're dealing with a designation of Marduk as the heir as "Lord of the Earth," a lineage and heir of Marduk, being Nabu.

And in the Sumerian tradition, none of—with the exception of Enki, the Marduk lineage is not observed. And so we see Marduk and Sarpanit, and Nabu and Teshmet, being primary "god–goddess" divine couples, represented as patrons of Babylonia—as opposed to the cults of Inanna-Ishtar and Nanna-the-Moon-god and these other former Sumerian methodologies.

It's in the *Enuma Eliš* that this "power" is essentially, officially, passed to Marduk, and is given the basis—which is what gives the basis for a Babylonian tradition and a Babylonian paradigm; because it indicates that Marduk will volunteer and be the hero on a condition that the Anunnaki Assembly will recognized him as "Chief of the Gods" upon his success.

And so when Marduk approaches the Law and is able to usurp the—or relinquish—the Tablets of Destiny from Kingu, and with that authority conquered the, basically, the true understanding of "Cosmic Law" and thereby Tiamat. He is given the position of—for the Babylonian Mardukite pantheon—the "King of the Gods"; and not that he is the original "Chief" or "Self-Made" or that there were no former ones, because Marduk is the son of Enki, son of Anu, and by that direct lineage, he is now—basically takes World Order and the authority for Cosmic Ordering.

This is what is set down in the remainder of the *Enuma Eliš* and, basically, the authority that is taken by Marduk—both the Tablets of Destiny and all of the Divine Decrees, the Divine "ME" discs or tablets or artifacts or pieces of information that basically represent the sovereignty of the Universe. And so what we're finding here when you examine it —and you know, again, this kind of encroaches on higher level understanding—but we're talking about beings that are basically coming into *this* "Physical Universe" and are able to structure and order it from the *outside*—and set these systems up, and who knows to what extent these Anunnaki figures, what this a representation of.

We know that *this* universe is a mirror or a lower condensation of *another* universe, which even in and of itself is not the absolute original form or even the position of Self—that we have descended through multiple universes. We can assume that the Game-play, the Systems, on which these universes operate are for the most part similar—particularly anything that regards a "Beta-existence." And *this* "Physical Universe" is obviously not the *only* "Beta-existence," it's simply the local system or the local "Cosmic Order" or what have you—or Solar System, a local part of the galaxy. Even beyond this universe—whatever has been partitioned as the continuity of *this* "Beta-existence"—we know that there are others.

We can assume, just as we have today, we have those that are working at this material to understand it to both, elevate individuals and others that are using it to create lower considerations of further and further degrades universes to occupy, that we can assume that there were exceptionally Actualized and "higher-minds" and beings in charge, and those with the ability to command various, you know, parameters of Creation.

In interpreting the origins of, for example, the Anunnaki—whether we're dealing with something as material as coming from another "planet" or another "solar system" or even another "galaxy"—that they are, you know, we don't want to get too lost in who and what these are. We know that at higher levels of Systemology reasoning we can break down our fragmentation of history and then later, in Grade-III for example, our fragmentation of associative knowledge and emotional reactivity, that there are higher points of knowing and realization that we can access.

However, at Grade-II, again, we're delivering in *this* essence, the Master Course to Master-level—those with all Grade-I through III understanding, before even beginning to deliver or administrate anything; but we're not trying to lose anybody along the way—we don't want to lose our Seekers along the way when impressing too much of the higher level Systemology and high level realizations when at a surface level we're simply extending what we already did in Grade-I in exploring various writings, various ceremonies, rites and texts and teachings, that have survived from various streams of the Ancient Mystery School—whether they be through the Western Magical Tradition or specifically Druidism or what have you.

Here, we are going back farther, we are extending back to the Ancient Near East; and before trying to blow your Seeker out of his body, we're simply taking examination just to the same extent that we did with the stuff from the last 2,500 years and going a step farther, and looking at the traditions verbatim, the history, the way it was presented on a surface level as a national religion—and then being aware, for example, with Mardukite Zuism and our new evolutions of Systemology that there are individuals such as you as a Master relaying such information to Seekers and initiates at gradients along the way, that there is obviously a difference in understanding the *esoteric*, the inner understandings maintained by the priesthoods or maintained by the original authors, or the oldest inceptors of some of these traditions and knowledge and sciences, that is different than the *exoteric* relay that is given as, for example, just a common communal societal tradition—as part of its culture and stuff.

A lot of the themes and icons sometimes are simply a way in which cultures began to identify with themselves and it tied them together and there (were) many levels of understanding applied—or available or accessible—concerning what that was representing.

For some, you know, "neopagan" or "pagan" lifestyles might just be a fancy way of celebrating various "loud" customs or getting in touch or some "inner self" or "primal what-have-you"—everyone has their own reasons, I guess.

But when we examine origins and we start tracing this stuff back, the farther back we get, the more intricate we get, in terms of just how significant and powerful some of this iconic imagery really was in what it represented; and this was not necessarily understood equal to all any more than the available bodies of knowledge that we have today are understood equally by all.

Even though any individual might have access to the same "books"—the same print on paper—even that is no guarantee; just having is no guarantee to the level of comprehension that's gonna be taken from that. We're gonna see that in any society. And so, each is gonna only really understand to the level and degree that they've arrived to.

For our purposes, we're simply looking at Grade-II as it was intended in its original formation as being the backbone origins behind, for example, the Western Magical Tradition, a lot of the systematization of today's society, a lot of the things we take for granted.

That's what it really evolved from. The fact that it's *become* this entire body of knowledge, the "Mardukite Core," the subject of "Mardukite Zuism," the subject of "Mardukite Systemology"—this is just what ended up happening [*laughs*]; it wasn't the original intention; it was a necessary evolution of what can happen when Self-Honesty is applied to these explorations.

And so, honestly, when you go through this material, you will discover many levels of understanding regardless of how many further "Grades" an individual takes it.

Every time you work through this system of knowledge, more of it comes together, more of it becomes complete as a picture—as a paradigm. It's incredibly new in the essence that the closest that most individuals have gotten up until the efforts of the Mardukite Research Organization—in terms of the Ancient Near East—has been Egypt.

Egypt has been far more accessible, in terms of its artifacts, in terms of its explorations, in terms of how many hundreds of years we've both known of it and being studying it or had interest in terms of human consciousness or even at an academic or intellectual level.

So when we're dealing with Mesopotamia—and we're gonna get into more of just the basics of what Mesopotamia is, and the highlights, so it has some kind of framework, some kind of point of origins in terms of your relay of it as a course—we're gonna get into that here. It's important for us to kinda clear the slate a little bit and understand that we *are* dealing with very ancient unfamiliar territory here.

And even though Mesopotamia may exist today, for example, where the country of Iraq is, it's important that a Seeker is able to separate these ancient studies—from thousands and thousands of years ago—from the politics and all of the, kind of, biases and news and such that have been attached to that area as a result of what's taking place today—the people in power and all of the wars and stuff that has been taking place in more modern times—because we are dealing with a completely different population now. And this Mesopotamian lore has been lost for a very long time and is not at all what is actually being revived in those areas; in spite of the ruins and some of the World Heritage sites that are accessible there.

[*So, in the next lecture, before we close out the day, I think it's important that we just get a good overview of what we're dealing with—in terms of Mesopotamia—and then tomorrow, we will spend the entire day digging out just about everything we can from the ancient desert sands of Mesopotamia.*]

: LECTURE 28—ANCIENT MESOPOTAMIA :
(September 24, 2020)

Now that we've adequately introduced Grade-II material, what we're gonna be covering, and kinda got you familiar with the concepts of Zuism—we've talking a little bit about what the Anunnaki material is, the cuneiform, the tablets; even the Babylonian "Epic of Creation." I think we've set up Grade-II pretty well. We might as well just dig *right* in to Ancient Mesopotamia now.

As you can see, the Grade-II material—the Route of Mesopotamia—this is a thousand pages of collected material over a decade that we're just gonna go through the highlights of and the specific points in the Mardukite Master Course a broad understanding of not only Ancient Mesopotamia, but the Mardukite Tradition within it; and *that* combined with the certainty and familiarity with the materials to give you the confidence to be able to reference exactly all the points-of-fact that we're getting into here.

Of course, the first point, of course, being, as you know, "Mesopotamia" is the "land between two rivers" according to the Greek language classification of it—the land between two rivers: the Tigris and the Euphrates. This concept, academically, we'll explore because it's a point made in the "Ancient Mesopotamia" material, is that the idea of studying "Assyriology" academically—the idea of, basically, culminating any and all Mesopotamian or cuneiform-using cultures under the academic study of "Assyriology" is actually wrong.

That classification is only because the original tablets that were discovered at the Library of Nineveh were written in the Assyrian language, and as a result, scholars and historians began to actually associate the entire pursuit of anything regarding Mesopotamia as "Assyriology." And that's something that we *don't do* in [*laughs*] the Mardukite Tradition; but we point that out as a matter of fact, because if you look at the Ancient Near East studies and the way it's classified at some of the various Universities, you'll see it as "Assyriology."

Now, though Mesopotamia is set to designate an area between the two rivers, in most cases the actual "Empire" of the ruling King usually extended far beyond that. So, you know, it extended as far as Egypt, as far as today's Israel, out to the Persian countries, you know, all around. And so, again, dealing with Mesopotamia, we're treating essentially the entire Ancient Near East for a given period of time—and most of the actual settlements—most of the cities—actually were set up and situated and cultivated near the rivers, near the two rivers.

As much as Egypt was a vast land and providence in terms of a Kingdom, most of the activity you see there is actually around the Nile River. And so, in these kinds of cultures— the desert cultures such as these—you see an emphasis on "Water" and the "Waters of Life" in relation to the survival of the people, their traditions, their mythology, and also what's considered "prominent." Whereas up in the northern countries you see more of an emphasis on "Fire"—the Fire Element—where they were using that to keep warm, they were using that to survive and even melt the abundant snow.

The two rivers extend down to a moist area in the southern part of Mesopotamia, which had more swampland, for example, as it emptied into the Persian Gulf. And it's interesting that over the course of the years—thousands of years— the two rivers have actually changed some of the way in which their course is run. It's evident that in ancient times when irrigation was being taught and used extensively and water is being diverted through various canals, that they had actually changed the nature of the river and how they operated.

Now, you see actually a change in the manner of the, for example, the shorelines and where different areas are designated based on the lack of the Mesopotamian culture—and the changes that took place over thousands of years being transferred from the original Mesopotamians into the, kind of, neo-Renaissance Mesopotamians and then the Greeks and then eventually the Arabs and so forth. And as time went on—up until present time—we saw less and less of the original traditions being observed, in terms of the management of the land.

And another function is the actual body of water—the Persian Gulf is actually shrinking all the time. And so more and more land is being established. The place where the ancient site of Eridu was—prior to the establishment of the Sumerian culture; prior to the establishment of Babylonia—Eridu was once at the, basically, where the rivers met the Persian Gulf at the time; and its now many many miles from where it is today, so that the Persian Gulf is actually drying up or shrinking. This is actually changed the nature of what you would see today [*laughs*] in regards to thousands of years ago when it was being settled.

As opposed to former civilizations and anywhere you see more—studies of anthropology come in and that type of archaeology as opposed to *ours*, because we're dealing with a time period that was still attached to writing and records, in terms of a civilization. So one of the things separating, of course, the nomadic and tribal cultures and the survival of the Human Condition prior to its systematization in Mesopotamia—one of the differences being Kingship.

You see this appearance of Kingship and the establishment of "rule" and the "Divine Right to Rule" as Kings being established by these Anunnaki gods to basically command in their stead. This is one of the things that separates and begins to change the culture; *that* in combination with its ability to establish city-states.

So, you see these elements—basically the systematization and codification of a civilization, where rather than those that were dwelling in caves, or those that were nomadically hunting and gathering, or those that sparsely were setting up small tribal communities; you see now, not only a rise of population as a result of, you know, these elements *allowing* the Human Condition to survive, but in the instruction of cities and the instruction of agriculture, the instruction of animal husbandry—all of these new skills and arts of civilization that, for our historical purposes, really kind of appear over night. This isn't really a gradual development.

Of course, the culture—the original "Sumerian Culture" that we call "Ubaid," which existed as the structure of the "Uruk Sumerians," when you start seeing the temples and the *Nanna* "Cults of the Moon" and *Inanna-Ishtar* and such. The more ancient times were still a period of cultivation and development—and that's why I say, by the time of the Babylonians, these systems were able to be codified, refined and established quite clearly.

The concept of this "Divine Right to Rule"—we discussed this a little bit in Grade-I because it involves the origins of the "Dragon Legacy"—this concept that these figures and this symbolism, as it was instituted in the consciousness, in the societal programming, how it really emerged and developed from the time of these ancient, very powerful ancient kingdoms, with very grandiose temples and their "National Religion," and then the establishment of the more familiar "governmental" institutions all throughout Europe; which, you know, we see more in the Western Magical Tradition and the appearance of the "Dragon Kings" and so forth.

The origins behind that really does begin in Mesopotamia with the Anunnaki being considered, for example, the original "Dragon" race; and then their selective genetic upgrading of specific lineages and then the instruction of (an) entire class of priests and priestesses to carry out the tradition and basically cultivate the civilization of Humanity.

So up to about the 3rd Millennium B.C.—we're talking now like 5,000 years ago—the land in Mesopotamia had been divided between, pretty much, the northern area and the southern area. And the northern area was known as "Akkad" and you see a rise of the Akkadian Dynasty; and it was the southern area that was actually considered "Sumer." As a result of the Akkadian Dynasty—the King Sargon—that you see a unification, finally, of Mesopotamia under *one rule* for the first time. Prior to that, each of the city-state areas were mainly self-governed with their own "king" so to speak—a "priest-king."

Although each of the areas—each of the cities—continued to pay its own patronage to a specific Anunnaki deity, and also maintained its own "religious" element in that respect, the kind of militant unification of the lands under one—as far as protecting all of Mesopotamia under one rule from outsiders—really emerged with the Akkadian Dynasty of Sargon; and it's also within the Akkadian Dynasty and it being the original "Semitic" language—"Semitic" culture—that you see the eventual designation of "Babylon" and the "Babylonians" as their own distinct culture.

Other "Semitic" languages though, also include Hebrew, Canaanite, Phoenician, Arabic and Aramaic—and so, you can see how, in addition to Akkadian and Mesopotamian being the oldest actually, these other ones actually stemmed from that and evolved in correlation with their own cultures and geographies as well.

The systematization, for at least 5,000 years, was under a particular "King" and this "Kingship" was observed by not only the "National Religion"—because the King was demonstrated to have "Divine Right" to Rule—but it also allowed the cultures of Mesopotamia to flourish, because they were able to be—with the systematization and the structure and so on—they were able to focus a little bit more time on arts and culture and not purely "survival."

And you see this really come into play during the, kind of, reunification or resurgence of these ideals around 4,000 years ago; and this coincides with the "*Age of Aries.*" Prior to that, you have the "*Age of Taurus,*" represented by the "bull." And in mythological connotations, the "Bull of Heaven" was represented by Enlil and the World Order of Enlil. And "Aries" is the zodiacal sign and symbol of Marduk.

This transition point, you see actually shift between, for example, Sargon—who was originally Sumerian, but became kind of the originator of, basically, the unification of Mesopotamia *enough* to *be* Babylonian. I wouldn't necessarily say he was the *origins* of "Babylon," but he *allowed* it to happen, by unifying the lands and *allowing* Babylonian culture, at that time, the room to establish itself under a "Mardukite" banner.

But this actually—I mean, this doesn't happen officially. Again, Sargon still operated under, basically, the Sumerian "Enlilite" Worldview. It isn't until—as far as historically, when you start to see another significant shift happen—which we consider the first great Mardukite King, being Hammurabi. And Hammurabi operated—he was one of the "Amorite Dynasty," which kind of replace the Akkadians as the Akkadian Empire started to fall—the Amorites take over Babylon and are guided there, allegedly—according to Hammurabi's own words—by Marduk; given the "hand and grace of Marduk" to go in and establish; given that the Sumerian Empire, basically, had fallen.

So, unlike being a great "War Leader"—it's within the Sumerian context that you really see the emphasis on material conquest and military—but unlike all of that, by the time of Hammurabi, you're dealing with "Mardukite Systeatization." So, you're really dealing with almost the origins of "politics" [*laughs*]—the codification and systematization of "*politics.*"

Rather than just be a "War Lord" and conquer peoples with "force," we're looking at an individual that actually *wants* to be—doesn't want to be feared—he wants to be "loved" by his people. And he's not setting up tyrannical laws to control them, manipulate them, or steal their wealth; he's trying to protect them and protect the order and structure of society: protect people from each other. This is where you see "civilization" really shape, because there you have the difference between the "civilized" and the "uncivilized" man. [*Laughs*]

And in the instances of Mesopotamia and the rise of the city —the "city-life"—you see the difference between a "citizen" and the "outsiders." And the "citizen" is given, you know, certain "rights" and is a participant in that society, in that culture, operating under certain moral guidelines; and by doing so, is participating in this system and the strengthening of this system.

Babylon as a city was the first in history to ever reach a population of 200,000. I mean, today, this may not seem all that incredible; but in ancient times, this—I mean, for all of the propaganda and quasi-historical "newspeak" that, you know, thrown at it from some "religious" perspectives— Babylon was not a "savage" "uncivilized" "bloodthirsty" world; it was the type of civilization *you* would *want* to be a participant in.

Kind of like, in some respects, for a really long time, everyone wanted to come to America, Babylon was the place to be —and it was the place you wanted to set up and be successful in; and it was a representation of this success of the Human Condition, in terms of its survival and its ability to triumph over, you know, its conquest of the Physical Universe —being able to command great building projects, to be able to sustain foodstuffs with irrigation, command and control of the elements—I mean, this was an amazing feat for the development of the Human Condition.

And if you look at, again, most of the infrastructure, the methodology and the systematization of ancient Babylon, you're looking at the precursor of, pretty much, everything that we have in place today.

Now, we're not going to get in too deep into the history—as far as the Master Course lectures are concerned, because that's a lot of material that you can pretty much just work through at face value the way it's presented in our materials. But, one of the key patterns that basically takes place is: there are certain basic fundamentals to operating in Self-Honesty; there's a reason why the "Divine Right to Rule" was instilled the way it was—the manner in which specific classes of priests and priestesses and certain lineages of "priest-kings" were given, essentially, permission within the paradigm of the people; the people participated with this, the leaders demonstrated why they were in their position.

In the Mardukite Tradition, it really is about what we're dealing with in, for example, Grade-III; it was really meant to gear—originally—toward the stuff that we *later* uncovered and brought out now, all these thousands of years later, as our Grade-III Systemology.

Unfortunately, given that knowledge and wisdom can really not be perfectly duplicated by the average individual—especially outside of Self-Honesty—we see a degradation or decline in Babylon occur any time its leadership is questionable, or has questionable ethics behind it.

This same concept rings true in, for example, the Western Magical Tradition or the Arthurian Tradition, where the concept of "The King and The Land are One"; and if the King is prosperous, then the land is prosperous, and the other way around. Any time leadership diverted from, or became aberrated from its true purpose, its true highest "Divine" purpose, in regards to the raising and elevation of Human society and actually the freeing of the Human Condition of the entrapment that actually took place as a result *of* these histories—the Way was lost...many many many times.

And each time a King, for example, would fail to observe the proper rituals—the proper ceremonies—to take his position seriously as an ambassador between the people and the "gods," the land would suffer—and the people would revolt. And you would see a change in power; and then it would take a *long* period of time before things would start to correct themselves again.

The great leaders of Mesopotamia, such as, you know, we talked a bit about Hammurabi, who set up laws to protect the people. And then one of the Assyrian Kings, Ashurbanipal, that was concerned about the loss of literature and the traditions of Babylon—because of all the changes in leadership from the time of Hammurabi—so nearly a thousand years later, he sends out his people to *find* every single scrap of cuneiform literature, all of the tablets that are available—the Wisdom Tablets, the Arcane Tablets—and he has them brought back to Assyria and, basically, copied (them) and copied in the Assyrian.

It was this collection of tablets—the Royal Library of Nineveh—that the archaeologists originally found when they discovered cuneiform tablets and cuneiform culture and cuneiform language for the first time. Because although it had always been alluded to all throughout, for example, Judeo-Christian scriptures—the Old Testament and so on and so forth—very little about Babylonia and Mesopotamia was really known. Even Assyria and so forth—very little was known about it, other than what had been, what was left over from biblical sources, Judeo-Christian biblical sources.

The effort of Ashurbanipal to preserve all of this cuneiform literature was actually of great benefit, particularly to us today. And it was very clear that he respected this tradition wholeheartedly—even though coming from Assyria—his efforts all surrounded the preservation of, specifically, the Mardukite Tradition. He dedicated—as the patron god of scribes and the one that gave the stylus pen to the scribes, to preserve the wisdom and begin systematizing knowledge —Ashurbanipal dedicated his entire library to Nabu, the son of Marduk.

Later, we see another Assyrian King that actually sets up in Babylon, preserves the ancient Mardukite Traditions, as Nebuchadnezzar II. And he dedicates—he stamps—dedications to Marduk and Nabu on *millions* of bricks that were used to pave a processional way for the "gods," and the rebuilding of the ziggurat temples.

So, the key figures in history—in Mardukite history—in Mesopotamia that stand out, the Great Mardukite Kings among them, were all very devout *Mardukite Zuists* (for all intents and purposes).

They were very adamant about participating in the literary tradition, the veneration of the spirit of that tradition as Marduk and Nabu, and their consorts Sarpanit and Teshmet, and the observation of these ancient Mardukite rituals —the simple prayers and the observation of the Akiti Festival, the Babylonian New Year Festival of the Spring Equinox —and the basic premise: the code of honor, of observing "Cosmic Law" and its applications to the governing systems of the material universe.

Those that operated in line with these—that understood them, that worked with them, that studied them the way we do in the Mardukite Master Course even—these were successful Kings, the ones that shaped history, the ones that brought a fruitful Empire and a prosperous Kingdom to the people and were venerated and loved by the people, not feared or hated as some kind of power-mongers.

And these are examples that we can find within the Arcane Tablets that point the way towards the proper—the original—systematization and also the *traps* behind it. I mean, not every King crowned at this point—I mean, this is now thousands of years into the history of Mesopotamia after the actual presence of Anunnaki gods has left because of the rise of human populations, and then the establishment of these lineages and these wisdom traditions in the absence of the gods, so that the people—the wise ones among them—would be able to continue this progress.

And of course, *this* systemology that originated in ancient Mesopotamia *is* simply that: it is the actual structure and development of what we have today. It doesn't mean it's good; it doesn't mean it's bad; it doesn't mean that everyone that's had access to this—just because they've been Wisdom Tablets of whatever—have executed the proper *actions* as a result of it. I mean, none of that's a *given*.

Just as a simple, as I've mentioned, just a simple read-through or a survey of all the literary work that's been developed, for example, the Mardukite Academy of Systemology, you know, reading it in and of itself doesn't guarantee that a person is going to reach all of these higher levels of realization from it. But we've not *hidden* anything; it's all there. I've just decided with the Mardukite Master Course lectures we would kind of emphasize and point out these key elements that we should illuminate.

There's plenty of details, names, facts and figures, which you can pick up from your own studies and using the materials at face value—but, once you know what to look for and have been given a clear set of lenses on how to look at it, you can form a much better opinion and a much clearer, more complete, opinion of how all of this developed and what you can do with it now—because obviously this is what we've based our Systemology on.

It is evident that a certain "class system" is being set up here—for example, between the figure heads, the Kings, and then the courts and the temple and then the priests of the temple; and the fact that the Nabu "priest-scribes," their tradition—I mean, they were some of the few in society that were readily able to read and write really well, and so it would be at these particular festival times, for example, the *Enuma Eliš* would be read out loud and often dramatically reenacted as like a play, like a pageant [passion] play, during the Akiti Festival. And all of Mesopotamia would essentially shut down for these Festivals so that everybody could participate and be a part of it.

These were planned annual occasions that, you know, they spent an entire year—there were obviously, just like you would have a committee or so forth for any local civic event—they would spend an entire year planning for this. Everything would be observed.

One of the traditions being—Borsippa, which is ten miles from the city-state proper, would be where all the "scribe-priests" and the "Order of Nabu" would convene. And each Akiti festival, they would actually procession the "statue" of Nabu from Borsippa ten miles, it would be brought to Babylon, specifically for the Festival event, to be reunited with the "statue" of Marduk. And we'll get into that—there's a whole series of things that take place and the dressing of the statues, and the dressing and the washing and the blessing and the presentation and so forth.

These were traditions that were observed as a part of ancient Mesopotamia—ancient Mardukite culture—and they established, essentially, the *first* religion; because prior to that you really didn't have a strict systematized "National Religion." Although there was an Anunnaki pantheon present in the former, pre-Babylonian Sumerian civilization, it was *not* codified and systematized as a "National Religion." It was really the elements of that—which later, when they are finally brought together—really end up becoming the basis of Mardukite Babylonian Tradition; and many elements of this tradition, when they are relayed in history and various books out there, they are often times misapplied to Sumerian as if all of this was actually Sumerian knowledge and the way that things were operated with the Sumerians.

It's really the case that a lot of the systematization—a lot of, for example, if you were to compare all of the magical correspondences and the elemental attributes and, kind of, all of the stuff we were talking about with "ritual tech," all of that was brought together and systematized for the purposes of an Anunnaki tradition, for the first time, in *Babylon* under the "Mardukite" tradition. And it was because of the fact that things were only loosely organized prior, that a new sound structured systematization could actually come and "take over."

And so, a lot of the "religious" elements were shifted to, basically, venerate Marduk and the Mardukite worldview in regards to the Anunnaki pantheon. Although the *Enuma Eliš* may have been presented in order to establish Marduk *as* the "King of the Gods," to give him the position necessary to *raise* a Mardukite Babylonian civilization.

The actual key messages behind that and the functional purpose of it remained sound—whether in regards to the cosmology, or in regards to whatever may have taken place with a different name under whatever, you know, former version that it may have had. But for our intents and purposes, when we are dealing with Mardukite Tradition—Mardukite Mesopotamia, its systemology and the evolution of Zuism—we are dealing with the cuneiform scriptural tradition as it was relayed by the Nabu "Priest-Scribes" *in* Babylon at least about 4,000 years ago.

: LECTURE 29—MESOPOTAMIAN MAGIC :
(September 25, 2020)

[*Alright, good morning. Is.. is it still morning? ...okay, well, good "soon-to-be-early-afternoon. So this is for the Friday lectures of the Mardukite Master Course, September 25, 2020. And I only got you for a few lectures today and then we break for the weekend and finish up—first thing next week—the remainder of the course. As I promised, this would be running for about ten days, and we'll still be able to meet our schedules and have plenty of time for other Systematic Processing and other things this weekend. If you remember yesterday, we crossed the threshold between the veils—the Gates—between Grade-I and Grade-II; and we're picking up in Ancient Mesopotamia where we left off last lecture.*]

When we talk about the structure of the Mesopotamian Systemology—the Mesopotamian tradition, particularly the Mardukite structure of ancient Mesopotamia—we're talking about literary traditions; we're talking about the social systems and the civic systems and beliefs and psychology, all being essentially unified a knowledge system that was codified with writing—essentially the purpose of writing.

This was the first time that "knowledge" was more than just experiential, more than just what you might go through if you were a hunter-gatherer, you're dealing with various aspects of survival, you're dealing with various elements of your environment, and a relationship there for your ongoing survival and existence.

Now, when it comes to the systematization of "writing," we start to see a codification of language in a way that actually begins to shape the way in which the Human Condition *thinks*. This is overlooked by most scholars; this is not really treated very deeply in traditional examinations of Mesopotamian "mysteries"—the religions, the traditions behind them—that "writing," the concept of *writing*, really changed the shape of not only civilization as we know it, but the Human Condition. It was a way in which the Anunnaki were able to, essentially, program and systematize what we know as the World Order—the Way of Things—what we *know*.

So this idea of *knowing*—the idea of "knowledge," the idea of "truth," "imprinting," "implants," "programming"—this is all in the background *of* the Mesopotamian tradition, Grade-II work—for the Mardukite Course—all of which ended up leading us to "Mardukite Zuism" and "Mardukite Systemology." I did not *invent* such concepts; these concepts are laying hidden essentially underneath the surface of what this ancient mythology—this ancient history, these ancient traditions—are actually demonstrating.

The Sumerian cities—particularly Babylon—was separated into districts. And so, you ended up having really two main powerhouses of a city-state: one being the Royal Palace; the other being the Temple. And for purposes of civilization, the material physical structure, for example, that which concerned trade, that which concerned protecting the boundaries of the Kingdom—military—that which concerned eventually carrying out the physical enforcement of, for example, in the Laws of the Code of Hammurabi and so forth—this was all connected to the Palace District, the King —this was in the domain of the King to be the material "Lord" of the Four Lands, the Four Directions, the Four Winds, the Four Corners of the Universe in the physical sense, the Earth.

Now, the real power behind Mesopotamia and perhaps even all cultures—as we go through not only ancient history, but considering even the effects of such organizations and "secret societies" and "cabals" and "fraternities" and such today—the real power kinda came from the Temple and the Temple District; of which, where the palace represented the seat of the King and the domain of the Four Directions—the

Four Corners of the material universe—the Temple was represented by a *ziggurat*.

A ziggurat being—these were made from clay bricks, and so they don't have the same longevity unless they are consistently rebuilt and reshaped and tended to, as for example what you see in Egypt and other pyramid-style constructions.

Now, when you look at the oldest pyramids of Egypt, you'll see that they're actually of a stepped design—they have specific tiers. And this is actually reflected very specifically in the design of the ziggurats—the more ancient pyramid-like Temples that were established in Mesopotamia.

The ones that specifically that represent the "Gateways to the Gods" or the manner in which Mardukite Tradition observed the "Seven Veils," the "Seven Gates," the "Seven Steps"—you see seven tiers on many of the Babylonian Temples, particularly the one dedicated to Marduk and also the "Temple of Seven Spheres" in Borsippa, which was the sacred Temple of Nabu and the home of the Nabu "priest-scribes" that operated about ten miles—eleven miles—from the city of Babylon.

So these ziggurat temples represented the stages of, for example, the Seven Grades—or the Seven-plus-One Pathways—that led to Infinity; the main spheres of existence. And these are each represented by one of the Anunnaki figures and corresponded to planets and whole bunch of other stuff. And of course in Grade-II—here we are in Grade-II—we're dealing with the Second Gate, the Second Step, the Second Tier, the Second Rung on the Ladder of Lights; all of this symbolism and even the concept of a "Stairway to Heaven" is all, essentially, derived from this iconic theme of "stepped-pyramids" as ancient temples.

These temples essentially represent the "magic" of Mesopotamia, and particularly the art of the "priest-magicians," the "priest-kings," "priestesses" and the wisdom keepers of Mesopotamia. And so, unlike some of the type of "magic" that's explored in Grade-I, the "magic" of Mesopotamia really coincided with an identification of not only the knowledge of the Gates, but also True Knowledge of "Cosmic Law," working along said "Cosmic Law," and at its deepest level we discovered, for example, the concept behind Systemology, which we now explore and are treating at higher levels; the actual backbone to what makes all of this function, and even to extent of systematization of world knowledge or worldviews, our experience of "Beta-existence" in this Physical Universe and our material lives.

We've seen how these have actually been structured, programmed—what we know, what we see—the parameters of the Human Condition; all of this taking place in ancient Mesopotamia with, essentially, a very clear knowledge of how this is demonstrated and how this is done.

Now, it's not perfectly duplicated throughout history, or we'd have no reason to have to go back to the beginnings in order to understand this—but, these key concepts and manners of tradition that were functional, the systemology behind them, the stuff that *actually* changes Human consciousness, was carried through into other cultures; whether or not it was understood what they were doing, whether or not it was executed to the highest optimal benefit of the individual, you know, that's another story.

But it is an effective technology and it's basically what constitutes the workability of any of the "religious" or "magical" systems or what we consider the "psychology" or even the "physics" or the "quantum" or "spiritual" aspects behind them—all of this was more or less sealed and solidified in ancient Mesopotamia in Human consciousness with the symbolism of these Seven Gates, Seven-plus-One Gates to Infinity.

Now, at a practical level, we know that the Anunnaki—as beings, operating physical conditions very similar to, for example, the Human status that you and I would use a "genetic vehicle" for—although they were able to be identified as separate from the average Human, they still operated, whether it be from an alternate existence, a spiritual existence, such as we do as an Alpha Spirit knowingly or not, they still resided in physical shells; they were still using genetic vehicles.

So, in addition to the cultivation of civilization, the Humans were used, essentially, to deliver the needs of the (quote-unquote) "gods"—these Anunnaki "gods"—and at one juncture in history, it's very clear that there *was* a representation of them. They weren't just statues—which they later end up being treated, as far as idols—they weren't just these representatives, such as the priest-kings that may have taken on names similar to the Anunnaki.

We're talking about beings that were very much physically present among the populations; and it's really only as the populations grew and the numbers of, you know, "human genetic vehicles" began to significantly surpass the number of deities and their factions—it's at that point that you start to see a physical withdrawal of Anunnaki or "gods" or "beings" all around the world; and this first begins with the temples—that these temples, at the top of these hundreds of feet high ziggurats, these temples that only the highest priest and high priestess and the god that the temple was dedicated to could even actually access. And so when the deities were still, essentially, making presences on Earth, they established these "homes" high above the surrounding population—not only for their own protection, but also the status that, of course, that provides.

So in the beginning, really, "magic" at this basic religious level is connected to a relationship that the "priests" had, and the "priestesses" had with the Anunnaki beings directly. They had the "Rites of Offering," which were mainly to direct attentions to the physical needs of the Anunnaki as they were there. Elaborate garments or cloths might be donated to them, certain metals, *lapis lazuli* was another, gold, alabaster—were all significant to the Anunnaki—and also the foodstuffs.

Of course, the Anunnaki were the ones responsible for educating the populations in the manners of agriculture; and did so on the assumption that, of course, they are going to be bringing this stuff to them; you know, teach them to farm, teach them to grow the food, and in return there was this kind of interplay of a symbiotic relationship between the populations and these higher beings. And the "priests" were, essentially, the intermediaries between them.

They would also establish the "Divine Right to Rule" with a particular "priest-king." However, the "King" really was subordinate to the *real* power behind the Temple. Because the Temple established its own wealth and its own power—its own collection of knowledge—even the people that worked there, the people that volunteered there, it was able to replenish its ranks very easily as a devotional tradition. Whereas "kings" may come and go; and their leadership mainly connected to the physical needs of the Kingdom, in terms of, for example, protecting the boundaries, protecting against invasion and maintaining physical infrastructure—the roads, the educational system; all of that type of stuff.

So there *is* a division of power and authority that was very strictly set down and adhered to, that allowed this specialized development of Human civilization—rather quickly. As time went on, of course, you start to see the same practices being applied in various other levels, for example, the idea of offering and sacrifice being used simply—in imitation—of the original physical needs of the gods, and later mainly serving—once, for example, the Anunnaki are no longer physically present—the offerings kinda keep coming, and they are meant to serve—although there is a representation of the deity up in the highest temple, the people don't realize at that juncture, all this time later, that it's really just statues and representations of the deity residing up in these shrines.

The wealth of the temple district continued to grow and grow and grow; and this actually led to, of course, fragmentation of the true purpose behind, for example, the priesthoods and the structure of the religion. And you start to see this degradation continue on into the "Classical Age"—especially with the Greeks and Romans and then into the types of traditions that we see kinda surviving *from* the ancient world in Europe and even in "*neopaganism,*" where the concept of divinity—gods and goddesses—the truth behind all this mythology, the origination of religious and human levels of "magic"; they've kind of deteriorated into what we actually study in Grade-I. And even our presentation of Grade-I far surpasses the type of relay—that type of magical instruction—from other sources.

Now, "Anunnaki Magic" or the Tech used specifically *by* the Anunnaki—the highest classes—for example, Marduk was the first "magical initiate" of Eridu, which was Enki's prehistoric—former to the establishment of Uruk Sumerian Tradition or Babylon, Enki resided in Eridu and the "magic" there would be considered something akin to the "occult sciences," "Systemology," the combination of the "physics," "genetics"; virtually all of the knowledge systems you might fragment this physical universe into, was within the domain of Enki.

His son Marduk was the first initiate and then became the "Master of Magicians" for the Babylonian tradition—essentially becoming the "Enki figure," replacing the figure of Enki in the Sumerian Tradition. So, this is where we also run into—and we'll talk about the nature and identities of all the Anunnaki today—but this is where we also come into, for example, the Mardukite pantheon or the Babylonian pantheon as being composed of the "younger" deities.

Even though many of the Sumerian figures still appear, the figures of Anu and Enlil and Enki are pushed into a, like, a "Supernal Trinity" that is far and above the material systems. And so we see Marduk and Nabu, for example, appearing in the Babylonian pantheon, which is something unique *in* comparison to a purely Sumerian pantheon.

Therefore there is almost several types of "magic" that appear in ancient Mesopotamia—or "Magic Tech"—because, we have the common devotional "magic" and religious systems of the people as the common people would understand it; we have the "magical systems" specifically connected to the knowledge as was understood by the priest classes, as they understood it; and then we have the knowledge as was directly observed—and as passed down—from the Anunnaki themselves, as they understood it.

So, you see, we have these "three steps" of, kind of, how this became the type of traditions that we explore in Grade-I, versus those that were the originators of it and had a much higher level of understanding in its application.

By the time of the Mardukite Babylonian Tradition the esoteric practices are mainly the "magical systems" or "magical knowledge" that is carried by the priest-class—the priests and priestesses. And this is represented, by this time, 4,000 years ago, this is represented by the patron Anunnaki deity Nabu—and Nabu and Teshmet are the Mercurial, or representing the planet Mercury, and also the Second Gate.

We are dealing with—essentially, when we are dealing with Grade-II—the Route of Mesopotamia and the Mardukite Tradition—we're dealing with the Second Gate; we're dealing with the actual "Nabu" plane or phase or level of work; and it just so happens to coincide that we're dealing with the, particularly, with the Nabu-Tutu (as they are referred to) Tablets; we're dealing with the tradition of the scribe-priests and the legacy that was set down in writing on these tablets—all of which is actually dedicated to Nabu.

So, it just so happens to coincide for our purposes that Grade-II—the study of Mesopotamian Magic and the Mesopotamian Tablets that were preserved by the scribe-priest schools and classes dedicated to Nabu and Teshmet—this is actually what we are dealing with directly *at* this Grade.

When the "magical traditions" are practiced by the priest-class, the priests and priestesses are acting on behalf of—in honor of—these particular, the archetypal "High Priest" and "High Priestess" which is Nabu and Teshmet. They represent the archetypal Babylonian High Priest and High Priestess, in which thereafter each of those that was observed in the religious tradition, and of course the temple district, the class of humans given that same position, are doing that in the "honor" of.

And the tradition of Nabu—if we're gonna talk about "Magic Tech" in relation to Mesopotamia; specifically Mardukite Babylon—we're talking about this passage of power between a lineage of Anunnaki deities, where each was using the *other's* name or the higher power in which to invoke and execute the authority *of.*

We see this a little bit in "Hermetic Magic." We see it a little bit in the Egypto-Grecian traditions. We see it, kind of, into the Judeo-Christian "Kabbalistic" methods. But, when it came to the Anunnaki, it all came down to an authority—and we discuss this a little bit in Grade-I in relation to the power and tech behind Druidism; because it's the same concept; that it's by the direct relationship of—knowledge of—this symbiotic synthesis of "what is true about existence" that allows this to actually take place; any of this to be effective.

And in the Anunnaki Tradition, we're dealing with beings *before* even the traditions are passed to—for the humans and the priests and so forth—we're dealing with, for example, Enki and Marduk and Nabu, that were all trained *separate* as Anunnaki beings, from the type of delivery of this type of information—these systems—for the human purposes.

And so, in the "Invocation of Eridu"—which is one of the opening incantations used in virtually all Mesopotamian Magic—it basically is speaking from the perspective of Nabu, which would have learned such from Marduk. Marduk would have practiced "magic" for himself in imitation of Enki. So, he would have, basically, said, "It's not I that commands and directs these cosmic orderings, these forces and these energies and the power and control of authority in the physical universe; it's Enki. Enki, Lord of the Universe, Lord of this Earth. I do this in his name, by his name and his authority" and so on and so forth.

You see this kind of practice follow through in the—even the grimoires and stuff of the Middle Ages. In the "Incantation of Eridu," it's Nabu, basically doing a roll-call and saying, "It's not I, but it's Marduk, the Slayer of Serpents, the Champion of the Enuma Eliš that is commanding these forces of Nature; and it's not I, but Enki, the Father of the Magicians, the originator of the knowledge in Eridu, whose making these commands." And this type of tradition, you see, actually descends to all the way into modern "magick"—this concept of using these spiritual roll-calls of authority.

In another version you see these lines written: "I am the Priest of Marduk, son of our Father, Enki—and I am the Priest of Eridu and the Magician of Babylon." All of which are basically... whether or not you're looking at it as you, you know, making an effect or change or putting a call out there into the "Akashic Realms" or "etheric realms"—*or* more accurately, you are actually assuming and taking on this kind of change in consciousness.

The whole purpose of "Holy Magic" and "Transcendental Magic" being that *you are* rising through these "Gates" or "Veils" and piercing new states of Knowing and Being; where the one that's actually doing the changing, the knowing; the one that's actually projecting all this; the one that's actually having a difference in experience *is you*—*is* the individual. I mean, that's what's taking place; that's what's changing here.

An individual is *using* this most ancient "magic"—as we might apply different elements more systematically in *our* Systemology—to basically *shed* these layers and these trappings and implanting and programming and fixed points of view in the Human Condition in assuming what's referred to, for example, in "Ceremonial Magic" as the *godform*; being able to assume a higher point-of-view *exterior* to all the confines of the Human Condition and being able to *operate*, for whatever given period of time, at that level.

And this is really the point that a Master is working towards, no matter what semantic or tradition or practice they're using. Whether or not it's clearly understood, whether or not it's workably effective in delivering... this is another story. But, these are the *goals* for the last *6,000* years of "magic."

Yes, we are dealing with the programming and the conditioning of what it means to be Human—and the entrapment of the point-of-view of the Alpha Spirit *into* the Human Condition—but we are also dealing with those, at one juncture, that *had* the knowledge of how this took place and how this was happening and could [*laughs*] actually do some damage control regarding the way it was employed.

The other thing you see with religion, concerning specifically in Mardukite Mesopotamia, is the transference all of the power and authority of an entire pantheon of deities *to* Marduk. This is a little bit different than the "monotheism" that was later installed within the last 2,500 years. It began with a system called "monaltry"—and what it does is replace the concept of "pantheism," where you have an entire series of deities, each with their own specializations and so forth.

Now, by the time of Marduk—Mardukite Monaltry—you are dealing with something incredibly unique here, because these other identities are not obliterated; they're not blotted out as being deities in their own respect. But, what is taking place is Marduk is actually—and this is given in the *Enuma Eliš*—he is assuming all of the power and authority and control *of* the remaining pantheon, and assuming it under his *own* name as being the one that is able to deliver an individual *to* any of these other points; and becomes, essentially, the representation of *all* of Anunnaki knowledge, wisdom, tradition and the Ladder of Lights—the Gateway of Ascent—to Infinity.

I mean, if you want to know *why* we call it "Mardukite"—this is what it really boils down to; the actual functional structure behind ancient Mardukite Babylon. The fact that we also deliver various instructional courses on the history; the fact can we can also treat it as mythology; the fact that we can develop our own brand of Mesopotamian Neopaganism as Mardukite Zuism—are all, kind of, subsequent *to* the idea that we can treat this knowledge as a wholeness and understand it in a way that has not been delivered prior, especially in the academic world, archaeologically, the history that most people are delivered.

You can eventually go back and find these correlating points of shifts of power and the changing states of the outer environment and the conditions that are observable, but the inner knowledge and the practice of the priests and the priesthoods and the priestesses, the Ancient Mystery School of Mesopotamia that eventually streamed out into all these various currents of knowledge that we've been able to explore since—we're looking at the core of it; we're looking at the origins, the archetypes, that which was the *first forms* of these, which later was duplicated and copy-and-pasted throughout history.

So, when you're dealing with "ritual magic" or "Ritual Tech" that pertains to invocations specific to the Mesopotamian Tradition or the Mardukite Babylonian Tradition; again, the "Incantation of Eridu" is one of the staples of it, as is the—if you're dealing with the ritual, the ceremonial—the designation of space. There are references to calling in Anunnaki figures or having representations on the left side and on the right side, in the front and behind, above and below.

These are actually—this is the "Creation of Sacred Space"—*is* creating these "anchor points" and being able to actually "hold" in the "Mind" these points that would create—well, *we* use a box or a cube, because it's actually a little bit easier to work with—but the idea of the "Magic Sphere" or the "Sacred Space"; an individual is creating space, putting out anchor points, when they conduct effective Ceremonial Magic.

And this is often represented, arbitrarily now, with invocations of the "Four Watchtowers" or the "Four Elemental Gates" or "Directions"—but, what's really intended to be taking place is the actual creation of *space*, personal *space*—a personal Universe—and the command and control over the mental imagery and the energy flows therewith, as directed by Self.

Now, this is something that, you know, you start working with at Grade-I, we're now treating it at Grade-II—it doesn't change as you work up through the Grades. The amount of certainty, the amount of specific—the fine tuning of these skills—as we work up, this is essentially the effective components that help lead towards, you know, this higher "Ascension"—*if* you're using "Ceremonial Tech."

There are several other ritual elements, such as the "Blessing of the Waters," the "Conjuration of the Fire," the lamps, the cauldrons, the candles—anything that you're dealing with; and then, of course, dealing with any kind of invocations, planetary associations, *etcetera*, with the Anunnaki figures directly.

And so, in addition to—for purposes of Mardukite Zuism—in addition to our abridged version, "*Anunnaki Bible: New Standard Zuist Edition*," which gives all the Arcane Tablets and the scriptures and so forth, the matching pocket hardcover of "*The Complete Book of Marduk by Nabu*" actually includes all of this type of information: the actual—the incantations, the prayers, the way in which you might enact the tradition that is only observed or alluded to from the scriptural tablets themselves. And, of course, all of this material is found within the Grade-II Master Edition textbook, which is "*Necronomicon: The Complete Anunnaki Legacy*" as it was compiled from all of the other texts that we used to go into that.

So, those are the main points of "Ritual Tech" as it applies to Mesopotamian Magic concerning personal dedications, personal invocations, personal prayers and petitions to the deities—and also the similar aspects of that when it was brought to the temple; when all requests were mainly brought to the temple and it was basically up to the priests and the priestesses to make petitions to the deities and supplicate them with these various incantations and invocations and rituals at the "Altars of Offerings"—and so on and so forth up the "ladder" of the spiritual hierarchy.

: LECTURE 30—THE SUMERIAN ANUNNAKI :
(September 25, 2020)

So, I promised we'd go through a roll-call of the Sumerian Anunnaki as they're observed in the Mardukite Babylonian Tradition. And there's many sources of this that you could use for courses—or for your own understanding. There's the *Babili Text*, Tablet-B, that's found in *"The Complete Anunnaki Bible"* or *"Necronomicon: The Anunnaki Bible."*

There is some brief information given in *"The Complete Book of Marduk,"* which runs parallel with—that was released alongside *Liber-50*, which mainly was a treatment of *"Sumerian Religion"* and is also in the *"Gates of the Necronomicon"* anthology, that really broke down the mythology of the Mesopotamian Tradition and all the figures of the Anunnaki.

All of this information is, of course, contained within the Grade-II textbook: *"Necronomicon: The Complete Anunnaki Legacy,"* the hardcover 2020 Master Edition—and we'll just kinda go through and hit all of the main points of these figures; give ya a good round understanding of the Anunnaki, what they were in this 6,000 year old literary tradition in ancient Mesopotamia—and you'll be able to make parallels on your own of how they correlate with *other* Celestial Mythologies from cultures around the globe.

So, if we work from a descending order—and we start with the Supernals—"Anu" or AN, he's given the position of "Father in Heaven" in both Sumerian *and* Mardukite Tradition in Babylon. He is the father of Enlil and Enki and therefore—since all members of the Anunnaki pantheon are coming from either a lineage of Enlil or a lineage of Enki, he's treated as, you know, genealogically as the "Father of the Gods." Between the two, we have "Enlil" and "Enki" as his sons, which represent the other two figures of the Supernal Trinity.

Now, Anu is given the domain of "heaven"—and the "House of Anu" is actually the original name for the planet, we say "Ur-a-nus" or "Ur-Anu," you know. It's literally still *in* the name of the planet. And so, he represents that in addition to being the "Father" of the two lineages and, of course, the Anunnaki in some respects.

"AN" is named for the name "heaven," "god," the "spiritual zone"—he's named for that. So it's one-to-one with. We have AN, the direction of the spiritual existence, the direction of the Spiritual Universe, or the Alpha-Existence in Systemology; and then we have a figure Anu—or "AN" in Sumerian—to represent this and simultaneously being the "Father of the Gods," being the father of these two lineages.

Now, it's assumed that he was in control, of course, of both factions of the Anunnaki; one being the Anunnaki—or *Anunna-gi*, which is how it was spelled by the original Sumeriologists—this pantheon of gods has been translated by Zecharia Sitchin to mean "those who came from heaven to earth." And technically you *can* actually break it down to mean that. However, for the last 150 years of Sumeriology or Assyriology or Mesopotamian Studies, the name "Anunnaki" meant "those who decree the fates of earth"—and so, those who were responsible for directing the various channels and currents and rays of authority of what was taking place on Earth.

So, wherever you actually see "Anunnaki" translated as "those who came to earth from heaven" and so forth—that's actually specific to Zecharia Sitchin's translation of the term.

The other faction of the Anunnaki are these beings—these higher actualized spiritual beings—is known as the *Igigi*, and they're referred to as the *Watchers*. "IGI" being the Sumerian word "to see" or the "eye" or "to watch"—they use the same for both. And in using it twice—using IGI and IGI twice—it becomes "Watchers" or "those who see" or "those watching." It becomes a plural form of the term.

The designation of AN, the AN-KI, all of this—this concept becomes very prominent in the "spiritual systemology" of the tradition. So we have AN and KI being both the representation of the "spiritual" and the representation of the "physical" and then we have figures, names or deities, that have been—in ancient Sumerian—given to classify these: so the "Spirit of the Heavens" being "ANU" and the "Spirit of the Earth" being "KI."

However, the designation—the Sumerian—the cuneiform designation for "AN" basically applies to all deities; and we see it translated as "*Ilu*" in the Babylonian language. For example, *Bab-Ilu*, is *Bab* being "gate" and *Ilu* being the Babylonian translation of the concept of AN.

And so, the designation of AN or *Ilu* is put in front of a deities name wherever it appears in cuneiform scripture. This symbol, in cuneiform—in Sumerian cuneiform—is actually the "eight-pointed star" or the asterisk; and this is the same "eight-pointed star" that is used to represent the "cross" or symbol of "*Mardukite Zuism*" and also its systemology.

Further now, we have "Enlil," which is one of the offspring of Anu and becomes—he's the official heir of Anu in the Sumerian Tradition. Anu represents the designation—the numeric designation—of *Sixty*, which is the perfect number in the sexagesimal mathematics of Mesopotamia. "Enlil" is represented by *Fifty*—and it is that number—*Fifty*—that Marduk ends up usurping *in* the *Enuma Eliš* and in Babylonian tradition.

So, rather than replace his father Enki, Marduk is replacing Enlil and assuming, essentially, "Enlilship" over material existence. And Enlil—when we look at Anu as being the "Heavenly One"—Enlil represents the spaces between the Heavenly domain and the Physical Universe, or the planet Earth.

In the Mardukite Tradition and Sumerian Tradition, he's designated as the "Lord of the Command" or "Lord of the Airs"—and again, this shifts in Mardukite Babylon—this position shifts to Marduk. In the existing Enlilite Worldview, this actually becomes the Judeo-Christian *Jehovah;* Enlil does. And we actually see a schism there with the "God of the Israelites" of the "Old Testament" Judeo-Christian tradition, and Marduk, who is the "God of Babylon."

Now, Enlil was set to assume "Anuship" in lieu of, again, being the heir of Anu; and by the Enlilite Worldview—by the old Sumerian, pre-Babylonian, worldview—Enlil then takes on the position of Anu and *his* heir-son, "Ninurta" or "Ninib" would take on the position of Enlil. And so this successive tradition was what was intended to be observed, essentially, in Sumerian worldview—in a pre-Babylonian Sumerian worldview.

We know Enlilship—and this is the representation of Jupiter in the Supernal Trinity—in the Elder Tradition, the Sumerian Tradition, prior to Marduk in Babylon taking on this same position of Jupiter and assuming the number *Fifty.* So, there is the schism or the difference between Sumerian Tradition proper, versus Babylonian Tradition proper, in regards to Anunnaki is that: Enlil was to become the new Anu; Enlil's son (Ninurta) was to become the next Enlil—and so on and so forth with this particular stream or lineage of the pantheon.

With the coming of the "*Age of Aries*" and the rise of Mardukite Babylon—and the fall of Uruk Sumerian civilization and the Akkadian civilization—we see this shift towards Marduk; where Marduk is simply the deity that represents not only Jupiter, but all of the various streams that any of the previous Anunnaki represented.

Now, in the pre-Babylonian Sumerian original cultivation of civilization and so forth, Enki and Enlil are actually—they're bothers. They're both descendants of Anu and Enlilship is not being questioned at this time. So, the idea of the "schism" or the "division" between pantheons is actually something that arises with Babylon—the time-period after the Flood, especially. Whereas the antediluvian—or the original ancient Anunnaki tradition—Enlil and Enki are assistants in the development and propagation of the lands, of the populations and so forth.

It really only becomes an issue when during the period of the Great Flood and "The Deluge," we see the Anunnaki, basically, withdraw from Earth altogether—and essentially believe that the Humans are going to perish, that this will be the end of the Human race. And Enki selectively decides to assist one particular lineage and trust to them the "Arts of Civilization"—the Divine "MEs" (*that we were talking about yesterday*)—and make sure that the integrity of all the efforts that have been made to cultivate this planet are preserved.

And this is something that is not agreed to [*laughs*] by the other Anunnaki; they are *not* to intervene. Given that Enki participated in the survival of the traditions all of the Arts of Civilization in Mesopotamia, it's after that point—and the restart of civilization in Mesopotamia—that we see more of an emphasis on *his* lineage and the position of Marduk and, really, the space and room for Marduk to come in and kinda take over and usurp the pantheon.

For purposes of the planetary or Celestial designation, Enki represents the number *Forty* and is classified as the planet Neptune. His name in—as opposed to "En-Ki" which means "Lord of the Earth"—his name, alternate name, also is E.A., which means "House in the Waters." And as we said previously, when we were talking about Eridu, which was on the coastline of the Persian Gulf, where he resided and operated and was developing the "occult sciences" here on Earth—

and so he was given that title: "He who lived in the Deep" or "Whose Home is in the Waters."

Enki, of course, as "Lord of the Earth" has been considered—in alternate anti-Mardukite anti-Babylonian Judeo-Christian tradition—is referred to as, like, "Lord of this Earth," "Lord of this World" or "Lord of the Universe." And it doesn't help that his particular animal representation is the "goat," so we see—whenever you're talking about "Luciferian"-type "Goat-traditions" and the "Baphomet" and things of that nature, a lot of that seems to be tied back to Enki.

Although we—I kinda illustrate the key deities and gods and goddesses, you know, gender-wise as they are relayed strictly in the pantheon, it should be pointed out that these figures, unlike what we might see—later we see an emphasis on male deities and you see a flip-flop now with the modern witchcraft tradition and a total emphasis on the goddess; in ancient Mesopotamian tradition, genders were actually considered as dual parts of a wholeness and were treated equally.

So, Enki and Ninki are the two—god and goddess—representing, for example, the Neptune current and that element, or that aspect, of the Supernal Trinity. Prior to that, you have Enlil and Ninlil as the "Divine Couple" that represents the former head of the Sumerian pantheon that way. So, in each of these cases, you actually see examples of, kind of, an equality of deities, and they are both treated, and the prayers are always directed to both aspects of each of these currents.

But, it's interesting where in modern paganism you see a real emphasis, for example, with the Sun being masculine and the Moon being feminine, the original designation for the Moon in ancient Sumerian was "Nanna"—and "Nanna" was the "God of the Moon," whose name means "Who Shines For" and... well, actually *Namrasit*, which is an alternate—each of these deities has probably over a dozen epithets or titles for themselves, which rather than being a proper name for the individual, the roles that were taken were considered to be "positions."

And so these positions would be interchanged and there would be this ascent or graduation or promotion—and it was assumed that each individual was occupying a particular position. There was no illusion about what was taking place; each one was an Alpha Spirit assuming an identity-persona-program that represent one of the Celestial—or in the case of the Classical, the "Olympian"—pantheon of beings; each one allocated to a "planet."

So, "Nanna" represents the Moon—and this is something that you don't see necessarily as common in later "paganism," which emphasizes only the feminine aspects of the Moon. And then the feminine aspects of that being "Ningal"—the "Great Lady"—or "Nikkal." So, this was a prominent force; the Moon being a very prominent presence—basically the Sun-at-Night, which illuminated and went through its cycles and phases, from which you can chart time by, the "months" and such. Of course, "months" being named for "moons"—so, as a counting of the moons.

We're talking about devotional or ritual tech or the religion and so forth, the Moon also being representative of "Monday"—and so, on Mondays you could, for example, as presented in *"The Complete Book of Marduk,"* you could be presenting or petitioning or working with that particular current on Mondays and making your invocation, for example, in the mornings—or whatever regimen you're working with for that.

We also know that the lunar current is water-oriented; it has a lot of blue hues—when you're talking about the colors—silver, black, white; these are all, kinda, representations of the Moon in ritual. And then, of course, the Moon being a representation of the "First Gate" or the First Level or the First Rung—the level of "enchantments," the level of "magic and mysticism"—the first Grade that we explored in the Mardukite Master Course.

And when you're exploring the Anunnaki or the Ladder of Lights and the Planetary associations and all of that, it might even be helpful—kind of like we did with the Elemental Model—to take paper or poster-board or whatever, and basically make a diagram or a ladder or a stepped ziggurat-styled diagram, where you can actually plug in all the classifications of Anunnaki and planetary lore and so forth, for each of these steps, and kind of get a more complete concept of the pantheon.

Of course, when we're dealing with the Second Gate or the Second Veil or the Second Tier on this pantheon—in terms of the Ladder of Lights; the way that it's demonstrated on the ziggurat, which is the order we're going in here—we have Nabu as the Second Gate, or the Second Tier, and this of course being one of personal interest to me; one that represents, again, the Grade-II work of the Mardukite Core, the cuneiform literary tradition and all of that.

Nabu, as representing Wednesday and Mercury, is also considered a patron of now only the writing, but scribes, messengers, divination, communication—things of that nature. Nabu is not necessarily the type of Anunnaki that you would see as a direct descendant of the Sumerian pantheon. Marduk's consort is Sarpanit, and Sarpanit was "seven-times-removed born" [*laughs*] from basically the original experimentation of Enki, when Enki was working to perfect the genetic conditions of the Human being.

And so, this begins with the—we'll talk about Adapa—but this begins with Adapa, and seven generations from Adapa, we have Sarpanit. And this is a line directly descended from Enki; and this is not an uncommon thing to have lineages like this—to essentially hold the same dynastic bloodlines within the tradition. And so, Marduk and Sarpanit are both technically descended from Enki.

However, the reasons why this works—and this is one of the key points in the way the pantheon developed; the way they kinda cross-pollinated with one another—is that as long as the *Mother's* side—the mitochondrial DNA side—of a genetic being was different, you could actually have the same *Father* parenting lineage.

And then the consort of Nabu being "Teshmet"—where Nabu is the "Speaker-communicator," Teshmet is the "Receiver-Listener." And by the end of the Babylonian age, it's Marduk that's actually entrusting Nabu with the "Tablets of Destiny" and the Ancient Wisdom Tradition and the aspects that we'll actually—when we bridge at the point of the "Tablets of Destiny" material; because we pretty much treat Marduk and Nabu as primary figures for the Mardukite Tradition—the lore regarding them, pretty much, permeates throughout; not just specifically, for example, this one lecture.

Now, when we reach the Third Gate—the Third Tier—we're dealing with the sphere of Venus, "Inanna-Ishtar," "Queen of Heaven." And in terms of the gradient system, where we have Grades I, II and III, representative of the first three Gates of this Ladder of Lights—this Ascension Path that has been set forth—we're dealing with the aspects of Venus; we're dealing with the passions, we're dealing with love; we're dealing with all of the "emotional" reactivity and "response-mechanisms" of the Human Condition.

And so honestly, very few individuals—I once released a book way back a decade ago called *"Beyond the Ishtar Gate"* as a play on terms; because really, when it comes to the Human Condition, when it comes to what most individuals—even prior to the establishment of the Mardukite Master Course and prior to the establishment of the "Higher Grades" of Systemology, very few [*laughs*] have been beyond the Ishtar Gate, very few have ever passed the Ishtar Gate.

And symbolically, of course, we use the themes and allusions of, for example, the "Scarlet Lady" or the "Lady of Babylon" or this concept that: even if you get that far, you're gonna basically end up getting snapped right back into the Human Condition if you have not already released all the emotional connectivity, especially regarding Human relationships, you know, "sex" being one of the ways in which the Human Condition is "keyed in" very heavily; where your point-of-view and considerations of Self are snapped in very tightly to the considerations of being Human as a physical condition.

Now, when we're talking about old Sumerian—pre-Babylonian mythology—"Inanna-Ishtar" is one of the key figures, perhaps key "goddess" of that tradition, and she represents Venus. And the original Sumerian astrology and cosmology and pantheon and so forth—as it related to the material world prior to the Seven Gates of Babylon—really it was concerned with the Moon (which we talked about Nanna already), Venus and the Sun. So, the Sun, Moon and Venus being the cardinal points of Sumerian astrology, and of course, those three points being the most easily identifiable in the (night) sky without much expert astronomical expertise there.

In terms of the mythology, Ishtar is actually—although she is a Sumerian goddess—she's considered one of the Younger Pantheon, much like Marduk. Ishtar is the daughter of the Sun and the Moon in ancient Sumerian mythology. So, this concept, again, made it more accessible based on the most visible planets—and of course, being a key figure in regards to the affairs of the Human Condition; the goddess of love, the goddess of war, the goddess of emotion, the goddess of passion—she became very significant in most of the traditions that are derived from the ancient world.

She's known in other aspects as "Goddess of a Thousand Names" or the "Goddess of Ten Thousand Names"—whether it's "Isis" or "Aphrodite" or "Ashtoreth" or any of these various representations, she has appeared—she has made herself very prominent. And in terms of the Younger Pantheon, the original plan, prior to what took place—in terms of Mardukite Babylonian—the original Sumerian plan was that Ishtar and Marduk would be pair-bonded; that they would consort with one another—become a "Divine Couple."

And, of course, this didn't happen; and this would have been one of the points in which the two lineages would have been unified—in terms of the Younger Pantheon—but this doesn't take place. So, in regards to the Sumerian tradition, Ishtar or Inanna, pretty much becomes a central figure as a "goddess"—the patron of all the priestesses and so forth; and this shifts in Babylon where, of course, we observe Marduk and Sarpanit as the primary "Divine Couple" of the tradition.

So, where Nabu's number is designated as *Twelve*—which is significant to the ordering of Time and those energies—Ishtar is given the number *Fifteen*; and Nanna was given the number *Thirty*—being the number of days in a lunar month by the old calendar.

The Sumerian calendar observed a 360-day year; 360 being religiously the manner of degrees the circle was divided in—and with their sexagesimal—their version of mathematics treated the number "60" (and "6") the way we would treat the number "100" (and "10") in the classification of groupings. And so, in their form, *sixty times six* being 360, it was the perfect—formed a perfect number. And then beyond that—the Heavenly Realm—you had 3,600, which was attributed to, for example—if you're gonna... we don't deal too much with the Sitchinesque interpretations and so forth *in* the Mardukite tradition, but 3,600 years was a *sar* or the amount of time that it took "Nibiru" or this "Heavenly Planet" to make its full circulation or complete orbit.

I mentioned the Sun briefly in relation to the "Old Pantheon." In terms of the language and the writings, we're talking about the same name for "Sun" as is given to the Anunnaki figure that represents the same. And so, in ancient Sumerian, you have the name "Uttu" or "Uddu"—which is "Shinning One." And the Sun as it is observed as being "The Sun," we see that in the Chaldeo-Babylonian and Akkadian name (as) "Shammash" [šamaš]; and it could be "The Sun" or it could be the actual Anunnaki deity "Shammash."

And the Sun is seen as the "Illuminator" of all things—the Shinning One—and in terms of the mythology, we see Shammash acting as "The Judge"—the one that, like, would be weighing on the scales and so forth, concerning the affairs of Men—the one that illuminates or shines light on the affairs of men. And of course, this ties in justice, law, balance, truth—the whole civic division of the concept of Truth as it applies to the mundane world.

And his consort, "Aya"—which is translated to "Shendira" in Akkadian—it's the word for "Dawn." So, Shammash and Aya represent the masculine and feminine forms of the Sun—and again, we see an equality there, a pair, a "Divine Couple" representing the Sun, whereas in more modern forms of "paganism" again, we see the Sun represented exclusively as a masculine form or "The God" so to speak, with the Moon being the epitome of "The Goddess."

In many ways it's the "Laws of Shammash" or "Shammash as the Law-Giver" which is the source of inspiration behind, for example, the types of stuff we would see in the "Code of Hammurabi." It just so happens because—Hammurabi—we're dealing with a Babylonian Mardukite Tradition at that juncture; it's Marduk acting as the Shammash or the Law-Giver, which is the author of that text. And then in certain respects, whether we're treating Mardukite Babylonian Laws or their tablet codes—even in the *Maqlu Ritual*, as it was observed in Babylon—we see Enki, Shammash and Marduk being the key characters of the "magic" and tradition and the incantations.

In Mesopotamian numerology, Shammash is given the numeric designation of *Twenty* and it is considered that the Sun—and the divisions of the Sun and its timeline—is actually reflected in an individual's lifespan; or that it was the Sun—or praying to the Sun or invocations to the Sun, that we see individuals praying to be blessed with a prosperous and healthy (long) lifespan.

Clearly, you know, on a religious level, we can see that the Sun being very present—being a part of that ancient astrological form, being the Sun, the Moon and Venus—it's very accessible; it's the deity that we can see all day long. The Moon being, of course, the deity that gives watch at night. And of course, it's the observance of the "Cycles of the Sun"—the divisions, for example, of the "equinoxes" and "solstices" and the "Wheel of the Year"—that gives a natural observation point for *this* "Cycle of Life" or the "Cycle of Creation and Destruction"—the "Cycle of Action" that takes place throughout the Physical Universe.

Of course, when we're treating the Sun as the Fourth Gate or the Fourth Step—or Grade-IV—on the *Pathway to Self-Honesty* or the *Gateways to Infinity*, we're treating, you know, the Sun as that point—that center point—of essentially... not Self-Annihilation in terms of what is *actually Self*, but the "purging" of Self *of* all the artificial; everything that could be singed off.

You're passing through a Gateway that is a division point between the "lower levels" and the "higher levels." The Fourth Step being the "midway" point—and it's represented by the Sun, which also demonstrates that the ancients had at least *some* inkling that we live in a *heliocentric*—or "sun in the center"—or solar-universe-type model in this local part of the Cosmos. That this is the way the pattern—the systematic pattern—of the Cosmos was developed; because we find the Sun right in the middle of the model of the Ladder of Lights as we're moving from this physical existence into higher existence.

And so what it represents is essentially a purging of all that is *not* Self. Basically all the imprinting, the programming—all of the stuff that's been accumulated during this lifetime—the resolution of all the facets of the Human Condition that keeps one tied back to the gravitational pull of these "lower levels."

: LECTURE 31—THE ANUNNAKI STARGATES :
(September 25, 2020)

[*So, before the break we started our analysis and treatment of the pantheon—a roll-call of the Sumerian Anunnaki—and it seems for the purposes of the Mardukite Master Course that it would be well within the beneficial realm if we were to continue to that; make sure we complete that for today.*]

When we left off, I believe we were talking about Shammash as the Fourth Gate; of course, representative of the Sun—and then of course, for ceremonial purposes, obviously connected to Sunday.

So, then when we move onto the Fifth Level—the Fifth Gate or the Fifth Veil—we're dealing with Mars; and essentially, on an energetic level—cosmologically, all aspects of that—between Mars and the Sun, we're dealing with essentially this spiritual barrier or the "Wall of Fire" that separates the —*all* the aspects that are connected with the Mind-System, the Human Condition; even its fragmentation across *many* Beta-existence lifetimes.

There's a certain veil there that separates *our* existence *as this* type of "Beta" incarnated existence—and our point-of-view considerations here and from this spiritual Alpha "outer dimensions" that are free from the gravitational pull of the "Cosmic Ordering" of *this* more centralized local system *here* from the Earth point; the Earth point-of-view.

And so, between the Sun and Mars—Fourth and Fifth Steps—we have, again, what we kinda classify as a "Wall of Fire." It is an incredible spiritual shield or veiling between what the individual *was* as Self *prior* to *any* type of considerations of being entrapped *within* a physical existence, and of course, those considerations.

Now that's specifically a reference to, for example, the "spiritual" or "Ladder of Light" or "Gateway" symbolism behind Mars. Of course, Mars is connected to the Anunnaki deity "Nergal," which is a Sumerian deity—and of course, Mars in our traditional classification of planetary alignments would correspond to Tuesday.

And in some texts, for example, the *Erra Epos*, "Nergal" is not really a friend to the Mardukite Tradition—to Mardukite Babylon—and never gives Marduk credit or (his) due to establish, during the Age of Aries, the Mardukite efforts in Babylon. So he is always kinda considered the antithesis *to* the establishment *of* the Gateway tradition, the Pathway out, the Ladder of Lights—the Babylonian (almost) usurpation of the Sumerian worldview and an access point to where, you know...

In Sumer, we see the systematization and the fragmentation of the Human Condition to where it just begins to assimilate this low-level point-of-view of being attached to the genetic vehicle, and then with this Ladder of Lights—the Tower of Babel—the access point from the Mardukites, is basically considered the antithesis to where all the Sumerian aspects and original Anunnaki efforts to systematize Human civilization and everything was basically in servitude to the "gods" directly and to their own needs.

After the Deluge, when Enki and Marduk and these figures begin to take more precedence in the pantheon and in the traditions, the "Way Out" or the access or, for example, the motif given as the "Tower of Babel" becomes immediately attacked by the Enlilite Sumerians. So, you see a period of history where Mardukite Babylon is in constant, basically, defense of its own *access* to "release" individuals—or "free" the Human Spirit—to these higher points of realization; and it's being thwarted from all directions, basically, being stuck in the heart of Enlilite territory there in Mesopotamia.

The rise and fall of Babylon—multiple times, because it was

reconstructed and re-surged at least twice—is not given one-to-one as fact in the Judeo-Christian concept of the "Tower of Babel."

This idea of trying to build a tower to reach God, or that God came down and smite them and separated languages and so forth—the confusion of languages—these are all vast simplifications and allusions that are preserved in Judeo-Christian lore, which was set down thousands of years *after* the fact; really has very little to do with what Babylon was.

I mean, keep in mind Babylon and Egypt and Canaanites and all this stuff—Baal worshipers and all this—they are *all* basically treated as "outsiders" in Judeo-Christian scriptural texts—the Old Testament and so forth; generally demonized, generally treated as the enemy. And of course, this is just a certain cultural bias that's left over from, for example, when Nebuchadnezzar II ordered the exile of Jews from Jerusalem for failure to pay tribute that year—things of that nature.

That's where you start to see a lot of these biases really enter into the scriptural texts and the religious connotations that are held by *most* of the world—I mean, if you consider, you know, the Judeo-Christian system and Islam and all of that stuff, you're dealing with a predominantly "Enlilite" faction of society that's become prominent, with Mardukites being really this minority—and yet holding on to some of the most ancient truths, most ancient writings, unaltered information, before it had been changed and altered; being selectively taken by opinion and so and so forth, in order to shape the mythologies of all these later traditions.

Mythologically speaking, you know, we associate Mars and Nergal with "war," but really it was about "destruction" and the "chaos" of that—where you might have one end of a lifecycle about "creation" and another part about "change," here you are finding "destruction" blatantly; and so, the name "*Erra*" is given as a title for Nergal—in the *Erra Epos*—which concerns the destruction of Babylon and his specific attempts to, basically, bring the system down... for no other purpose than sheer jealousy; acting on his own will.

And there are several points where he is used to carry out the "destruction"—for example, which you find in "Sodom and Gomorrah" and things that do appear in remnants of the "Old Testament." This is the figure that does that; and coincidentally, his consort—or rather, perhaps, in terms of power, the consort *of*—"Ereshkigal." And Ereshkigal is the "Goddess of the Underworld," the "Goddess of Death," the "Goddess of the Shadows." And so, you have Nergal as the "Annihilator," "The Destroyer"—almost like an "Angel of Death"—basically delivering those down to the Underworld.

Although the *real* cosmology and religious tradition and beliefs is a *very* gray area when it comes to our analysis today of ancient mythology. It's very obvious to us that in—much the same way as, for example, "Old Testament" Jews or followers or whatnot in that tradition, it was assumed that Jesus would come and open the Gates of Heaven and open the *access way-point* in which beings would be able to Ascend and free themselves from the trappings of the Human Condition. Prior to that, it was assumed that they were kind of hanging out in some kind of "Limbo" (so to speak), as far as the Judeo-Christian tradition is concerned.

So, as an alternative to this "Land of the Dead" or whatnot, the "Ladder of Lights" paradigm really suggests that there was a deeper understanding—or a higher spiritual realization—of what was *accessible* concerning the Human Condition and the Human Spirit.

It's also important—I point out here that, we're not talking about "good" and "evil." We're talking about "creation" and "destruction" and handling various aspects of the experience in the Physical Universe and "Beta-existence." And ironically, when we talk about Ereshkigal, who is the "Goddess of..." essentially "Underlands"—or "Land of the Dead" or such—her *sister* is actually Inanna-Ishtar.

And in the epic, the account—"*The Descent of Inanna-Ishtar*" or "*The Crossings of Inanna-Ishtar to the Otherworld*"—or the "Underground," or the "Underworld"; there are so many different applications [*laughs*] to what we've referred to as this "Other," these two, they actually end up being pitted in combat against each other; I mean, wrestling about on the ground and so forth.

We know there is definitely some politics involved with the Anunnaki. Most of what I've relayed, for example, in *Liber-50*, which was first released as "*Sumerian Religion*"—it's also available in paperback as "*The Sumerian Legacy*" from *The Joshua Free Imprint*—but we included in the "*Gates of the Necronomicon*" anthology and it's, of course, within "*Necronomicon: The Complete Anunnaki Legacy.*"

Now these accounts are based on a collected understanding of looking over all the tablets—looking over all the incantations, the various titles that these individuals carried and their relationship to one another; because unlike, for example, the Epic Sagas and some of the Philosophical Accounts that we can pull out of the "Classical World" like the Greeks and Romans and from Western Europe and so forth, most of our understanding is *compiled*; most of our understanding is by examining all of these materials and then putting out this overlay of how all these figures fit together. There's really no tablets that strictly define that or give you a catalog like you would find in these, for example, more recent "grimoires" and "catalogs of spirits" and pantheons and various Magical Schools.

A lot of this is knowledge that had to be derived—it had to be developed—of which we can later give this more common overview *of*, but that's why it took so many years and why so many pages and so much development and research to bring it to this point, because nowhere could we find it this clear cut and dry. And so the Mardukite Chamberlain work—the "Mardukite Core"—that composes the Grade-II textbook is a reflection of that work.

And then of course, now, we've seen the evolution of it as Mardukite Zuism and Mardukite Systemology, but for thousands of years it lay dormant. You know, up until recently, in the last decade, very few were examining this higher echelon of knowledge in connection to it.

Now, Marduk is, of course, the name and representation of Jupiter for the Babylonian Mardukite Tradition—he's the figure, of course, for which the whole tradition is named for. And we cover—I mean, he comes up a lot, much like Nabu, because of its ties specifically to Mardukite Babylonian Tradition. This is a name and figure that comes up quite a bit—and given that the *Enuma Eliš* is actually the basis of the Babylonian Mardukite Tradition, the "Epic of Creation" and his "Cosmic Ordering" and his assumption of the "Fifty Names," which is of course the "Fifty Gates" or "Fifty Divisions"—The "49+1" between the Physical Continuity of Beta-existence *and* out to Infinity. All of this became assumed under the Mardukite Tradition.

He doesn't really appear very much in the Sumerian texts; in fact, Marduk being a Babylonian name for him—but in some of the older versions he's named "Amarutu," which means "Light of the Sun on Earth" or sometimes equated to, for example, the "Son of the Sun" or the "Solar Calf." He was kinda tied into almost become a representation or the next position holder of Shammash. Even in Babylonian Tradition, he pretty much assumes that role anyways—but, for purposes of what we classify…

In 2160 B.C., we enter what is called the "*Age of Aries.*" And the reason why there was so much confusion and conflict is that, although you can divide, you know, you can divide the sphere or the circle or the zone of the Zodiac—as it is a circle that encompasses our field of view—into *twelve* divisions, and each of those divisions being equal parts in terms of space: what each division was represented by was a particular zodiacal constellation. And this constellations are *not* all the same size.

And so, on either side of "Aries"—you had "Taurus"; you have "Pisces"—these are very big constellations that occupied a large part of the field—the zone—of each of those "Houses." That's where you get your "Twelve Houses" of the zodiac; the circle was divided into *Twelve*; just like "Twelve Months." And each of these zones occupied a particular "degree" or "arc" of vision.

But, the constellation of "Aries" is very small, so by observation, an alignment with that constellation only takes place for a shorter period of time than one could look out and go, "Oh, yep, there it is, the Sun rising in the zone of" for example, "Taurus, or the zone of Pisces," which just occupy a much larger "arc" of space and because of the amount of stars making up the constellation.

But from this point [*the Age of Aries*] on, Mardukite Babylon is established; and it is established by, essentially, *installing* into consciousness—into the mythology, into the worldview of the Anunnaki pantheon—the *Enuma Eliš*, or the "Epic of Creation," which basically fixed Marduk up at the height of the "gods."

Now, the Anunnaki creation of the Human form—the "*Adamu*"—is given in every version of "*The Anunnaki Bible*" that we've ever released. And the evolution from that, being that specifically among them, there was one that was selected and directly—basically, the genetics of Enki directly. And so this kind of cross-breeding takes place; and this is one of the reasons why the Anunnaki, kind of, have a schism between the Mardukite lineage under Enki versus the Enlilite Tradition.

Because it is Marduk—as head of the IGIGI in pre-Babylonian times—and then Enki, with the genetic upgrading of Humans and then the eventual cross-breeding with them, that is considered a blatant... blatantly against the will and commissions of the original Anunnaki Council and their conduct on Earth and the involvement with Humans.

I bring this up, because, "Adapa" is the one that—essentially, Enki ended up [mating with] an Earthling female that he had selected then; don't forget that he's involved with the genetic upgrading and programming and implanting of these beings—as the worker class. So, he selects one especially, and from that we have "Adapa," which gives rise to a different line of Humans that is now coexisting with the previous population.

But, this one [Adapa] is special—and is taken to Eridu and kept away and trained in the arts of, for example, the "magical sciences" and the knowledge of the "gods" and so forth, in Eridu. Now, seven generations after Adapa, we find Sarpanit. And Sarpanit being the chosen spouse of Marduk—and not just for the purposes of mating or so forth, or to produce an heir—Marduk, who at this juncture, is already giving up his rights, virtually, to rule in "Heaven" or to be a part of the previous alignment of the Sumerian tradition of succession, of which it was questionable that he was going to be anyways.

He decides that—this is where you kinda get that concept of, "well, it's better to reign in Hell then serve in Heaven" type thing; because, here it is, him setting up his own dynasties with the assistance of Enki—his own lineage of Dragon Kings; his own priest-class; his own tradition; and in doing so, he's also taking—although she was a direct descendant, in essence, of Enki, he's taking a Human female to be espoused with and she ends up being elevated to goddess status, of course, in Babylon: Marduk and Sarpanit.

It's also—if you look at the generations of Adapa on Earth from the *Tablet-D* series in the "Anunnaki Bible," it's also from Adapa, that in the second generation, you see "Kain" and "Abel." And "Kain" and "Abel"—these appear on cuneiform texts thousands of years before their appearance in any version that's attributed to the Judeo-Christian tradition.

And the division *here* between brothers, being that Marduk instructed "Abel" in Shepherding and "Ninurta" instructed "Kain" in agriculture; and then in the same spirit as what you've been kinda given in other versions; Kain kills Abel and is essentially exiled. And this idea of "Cain," the "Canaanites" and the "Vampyre Lore" and tradition that stemmed from that—which is, kind of, becomes a staple of the "Left-Hand Path" and a lot of other versions of Babylonian Magic that have stemmed out from there—that's where all that comes from. And it's basically the outsider's antithesis to what was taking place in Sumer at the time and even under the kinda proto-Babylonian generations from Enki and Marduk and so forth.

We actually treat—although it's not *officially* part of the Mardukite Master Course—five years ago, a faction of Mardukite Alumni got together and formed—it was kind of a precursor to any of the newer "Systemology" work that we have—we formed this group called the "Moroii ad Vitam." We *still* actually have available; it's called "*The Vampyre's Handbook*" and there's a collector's edition hardcover still available from *The Joshua Free Imprint*.

But, this underground group was actually working with a whole different *view* of taking all that had come before, and the materials—a lot of which we've already covered in the Master Course here—and looking at it from a different perspective; and also exploring the entire "Cain and Lilith" elements out of Mesopotamia and how they, kind of, evolved throughout history.

There's a lot of "mysticism" and deep "Spiritual Tech" that can be found—even in just looking at the "Arcane Tablets"—

looking through the materials of "The Anunnaki Bible," that portion—that entire collection of work, actually, reprinted *"The Complete Anunnaki Legacy"*; it's one of the main portions of the text. And, of course, if you're, you know, if you can read between the lines a bit and get a different take on it than just the literal, there's a lot of information in there that becomes the basis of later "Hermetic Magic" and the "Ceremonial Traditions" and a lot of what became a little bit more popularized in the Magical Revival within the last couple hundred years.

So then, of course, Marduk represents the "Gate of Jupiter" for the Babylonian Tradition, and the Sixth Level—or the Sixth Sphere—beyond the Fifth... the Nergal... Beyond that... So, now we're dealing with Jupiter—the Sixth Sphere—and we're dealing with a point in which, you know, in just looking at the *Enuma Eliš* and looking at the basis of the tradition, we're talking about "Cosmic Ordering," the "Ordering of Universes," the idea of spiritual existences—the fractioning of those—the way in which everything has been fragmented and divided.

The classification of "Cosmic Ordering"... you know, the perfection of the "Tablets of Destiny"—all these things, all represented at the Marduk (Path), Jupiter, a point of expansion, a point of solidity, a point of certainty, a point where the Self is actually reaching, you know, where it can actually say it's reaching an Actualized Point *from* Self; because beyond that, then we deal with—Oh, by the way, Jupiter, of course, being connected to Thursday, or what was named for Thor's Day... and, of course, Marduk and Jupiter and Thor—if you wanna look at that Celestial Pantheon then they are all connected. There is, again, a lot of similarities that one could draw concerning the various Celestial Pantheons and how they correlate, based on the planetary assignments of these figures alone.

So, when we move to the Seventh—and the final "Gateway" *of* the "Ladder of Lights" as it's presented, or the planetary system—we're now getting into Saturn, which is Saturday; and in the Sumerian tradition, this is observed as "Ninurta." It's really not even treated very much *in* the Mardukite Babylonian Tradition, to be honest with you, because once you're getting to the Sixth Gate of Marduk, you're basically using Marduk as the *access point* or kind of...

In the Kabbalah, they refer at that point to almost this "hidden back door" to the Tree of Life—basically, this access point where Marduk has installed a way of achieving—or getting to—*out* of this system or towards the Supernal Trinity—or to the Gateways of Infinity—using *himself*. And it's for that reason that Babylonian Religion became a very Marduk-centric type system and presentation.

"Ninurta" or "Ninib" or however—and in whatever tradition that this other figure—that this original heir or Enlil was designated, represents Saturn; and in that respect, also Saturday. So, there you have at least a brief run-through on what all the Anunnaki figures are as they appear in this tradition.

When we're dealing with the "spiritual" or the "energetic" aspects of—when you're getting to Seven, *Grade-VII*, or "Seven" on the "Standard Model"—the idea that we are actually going back to Self *as* Self. Doing so is basically to confront the "Shadows," to confront the "Darkness," to confront, essentially, *everything* that we have at that, up until that point, decided to turn away from or repress or *anything* that is otherwise, again, *not* Self.

And at this point, we're dealing with a point *beyond* the type of way in which we've been defragmenting in the past; we're dealing with the actual nature of *Self* at its Alpha Point of Existence as "I-AM"—standing at basically a "crest-peak" or "island" across a... on "Seas of Infinity," so to speak.

So now in ancient Mesopotamia—particularly on the tablets

—the idea of these Gates and the way that the Gateways to Infinity and the Pathway to Ascension and all of this stuff that we're treating at more of a systemological level, is understood now, is not necessarily the way it was given in ancient times. This is being treated as, basically, you know, for example, even just allocating these figures to the planets: they were delivering "religious"—a common person's "religion" as a "National Religion"—to the common individual, as a citizen.

It wasn't expected that every individual was going to know this higher upper echelon of knowledge; this is something that actually requires a "priestly" application to make effective.

And so, all throughout history then, you start to see this same work, for example, as it was turned into—for the purposes of the Ancient Near East—it survived as the Kabbalah; you see this Kabbalistic—it becomes "Rabbinical Knowledge."

It becomes where everyone is loosely aware that it *exists*, and you know, they can study it to the extent that they really understand it. It was really a select few individuals that had the esoteric and mystical and religious and spiritual understanding—a masterful understanding of this—in order to demonstrate the lower-levels of understanding for those that *that* was where they were at.

There's multiple levels of the delivery of Sumerian Religion —or Babylonian or Mardukite and so forth—and that's basically what we've done here, is we've synthesized for the Mardukite Master Course, this same academic level of instruction and the same pursuits and the same research that texts, such as you see in "*The Complete Anunnaki Legacy*" for the Mardukite Master Course of instruction; and then we see a completely different relay—more simplified, a more basic, easier to access entry point—as "*Mardukite Zuism,*" which is really an abridgment of the type of work that you would find, for example, in this large textbook.

So, the Anunnaki Stargate System of Babylon—this Ladder of Lights or Stairway to Heaven—that's proposed in the Mardukite paradigm—and this is really nothing short than the original methodology of "systematic removal" of the filters and programming and imprinting that really has kept Human experience—or the Human Condition—*from* the Self-Honest experience and the Awareness of the Absolute; and Infinity and "Cosmic Law" and the truth about Self, the ability to be... that the true nature of Self is a *creative individual* with *creative abilities*—and that most of this has been actually since been watered-down, even under the allusions of being a magician's art or wizard's art—such as we've seen and examined in the Grade-I materials.

And so, it actually—for the purposes of the Mardukite Master Course—we can actually move much quicker, we can actually cover more ground in less time, as we move up these Grades because we're simply *adding* to what we've explored and the various levels of understanding that were reached at previous Grades. So, we spend less time discussing Grade-II; also because of Grade-I having both the "Route of Magic and Mysticism" and the "Route of Druidism and the Dragon Legacy" connected to it.

But, once we know we have actually worked through all those materials—which for our purposes, would be everything, the first *twenty-four* lectures of the Mardukite Master Course—basically, it all sets up so that we can actually deal with Grade-II at a much more expedient level and at higher levels of realization, knowing that we've already worked through that.

And as you'll see, when we get into things a little bit deeper *next week* and wrap up the Mardukite Master Course, we'll be transitioning *next week* from Grade-II into Grade-III, with a *very* smooth transition regarding cuneiform tablets and "*The Tablets of Destiny*" and the *Enuma Eliš* and all of that—

and be able to cover that in, basically, as almost an extension course to Grade-II, because we're dealing with all the same familiar concepts and names and so forth that we're treating now.

And then as a result of that, we've been able to cover 6,000 years of nomenclature and semantics and cultural interpretations, we're then able to discuss Grade-III—Mardukite Systemology—at a much higher level and with greater clarity, having already covered *everything* that's led up to the actual literal development of the "Mardukite Systemology," which is, basically, the advanced spiritual tech *of* even Mardukite Zuism at Grade-II.

So, what I've been able to cover then, with these first series of five or six lectures for Grade-II, is essentially when you're looking at your textbook for this Grade—the "*Necronomicon: The Complete Anunnaki Legacy*"—we've basically been dealing with the *Liber-51/52*, when we deal with "Ancient Mesopotamia"; we've been dealing with *Liber-E*, when we are concerned with the *Enuma Eliš* and the structure of Babylonian Magic and the Stargates; and we've been dealing with *Liber-50*, in regards to information that we can draw concerning who all these Anunnaki figures are.

And so, that actually brings you up—I mean, if you're working it through the textbook and of course, there's a lot more details in there than what we've just brushed through—that gets you up to the point of where the main body of "The Anunnaki Bible" is positioned within this Grade-II textbook.

: LECTURE 32—THE ANUNNAKI BIBLE :
(September 25, 2020)

[*Okay, so we're at the final lecture of today. I figure we'd better close out today's cycle of lectures and the week that we're having—it's been a very intensive week. We've just covered the concepts of Ancient Mesopotamia, the use of Mesopotamian Magic, establishment of religious institutions, systems, the pantheon and Gate symbolism attached to the Anunnaki.*]

I figure we'll do a little preview [*survey*] of "*The Anunnaki Bible*" and go through, essentially, the "Mardukite Tablet Catalogue"—which has been released in multiple editions. In its complete versions, it's found of course, in your Grade-II textbook, "*Necronomicon: The Complete Anunnaki Legacy.*" It's also found as "*Necronomicon: The Anunnaki Bible*"—the 10th Anniversary hardcover edition; and then "*The Complete Anunnaki Bible*" in paperback, which just simply doesn't use "Necronomicon" in the title.

And then there's two times when we've abridged this. So, there's the pocket edition of "*Necronomicon: The Anunnaki Bible,*" which is in paperback; and then, of course, the "*New Standard Zuist Edition*" that has been released for the "Founding Church of Mardukite Zuism" in the new hardcover premiere edition—and that's also abridged from the complete tablet catalogue. So, we'll go through as it appears in your Grade-II textbook—"*The Complete Anunnaki Legacy*"—we'll go through the tablet catalogue of "*The Anunnaki Bible.*"

As I discussed before, as you know, "*The Anunnaki Bible*" for our tradition, is composed of what took many many discourses—many individual booklets that were developed in the Mardukite Chamberlains, the Research Organization—and eventually compiled into a "Bible," a complete "Bible."

Most of the material was developed in 2009. There were several editions and revisions and so forth, which were added over the next few years after that to round this out. And originally, it wasn't really an A-to-Z presentation of the (tablet) material; but as each of the cycles or series of tablets were designated as, like, "Tablet-A" or "Tablet-B Series" *etcetera*, the current editions of "*The Anunnaki Bible*" basically give these in sequence as they're relayed in that catalogue.

It's only been as a result of this "New Standard Edition" for the *Zuist* religion—this "Anunnaki Bible"—that is an abridgment, where I've actually reorganized the sequence of tablets to be more chronological, as if you were reading, for example, the way "Old Testament Bible" of Judeo-Christian scripture is laid out.

But, for the purposes of the Master Course—and most of the complete editions—the tablets are arranged in sequence, based on simply their titled; no other consideration being given here.

The "Tablet-A" series, we're being introduced to the Anunnaki—the developments of the Anunnaki on Earth—about how the IGIGI "Watchers" came down and were entrusted... These were originally, you know, these "high class of being" and here they were down on Earth digging out rivers and canals and doing all this physical drudgery—and it's at this point that they start to establish this idea that they should probably come up with an alternative, another race of being that's going to do this work.

At one point the "Watchers" even revolt; and so you see—just kind of like some of the Judeo-Christian, in the way it's relayed in terms of Heaven and Hell and these various factions of angels and Lucifer and all that—when you look at the more ancient texts that describe all these activities, there isn't as much of a moral classification about it; it's really all about pragmatism and "utility" in terms of what's taking place between these various beings.

The designation and classification of the Anunnaki and the Gates and the divisions is introduced in "Tablet-A"; and then in the complete versions, there's also excerpts from the "*Egyptian Book of the Dead*" to, basically, just show the parallels there.

And then "Tablet-B" we're presenting the *Babili Texts*—the invocations of the various Gates; the designations of the Anunnaki, the sevenfold system as we were basically discussing it in the previous lectures; and then again, in the complete versions, you'll see that there is the "*Coming Forth and Crossing the Seven Gates*" excerpts being taken from, again, the Egyptian texts.

Now, in "Tablet-C," we find—and this is we... I brought this up previously: the "*Crossing or Descent of Inanna-Ishtar into the Underworld*" is given as "Tablet-C" as the "Book of Crossings." And this is a lengthy narrative that basically describes Ishtar descending through Seven Gates, having to remove seven layers of clothing, of garments, of all the objects—sacred objects and regalia—that she carried; what represented her being the Queen of, basically, the "Lands Above," and having to relinquish all these to actually approach the Underworld.

In a lot of editions—or interpretations of this, rather—the purpose of it is to rectify the wrongful death of her consort, "Dumuzi" or "Tammuz," which is the individual she ends up with as a result of Marduk and her not, of course, completing *that* arrangement. And there's, again, "*Crossing Forth*"—and the "*Book of Crossing*"—from the Egyptian sources, spliced along with that in "Tablet-C" in the Complete versions.

"Tablet-D" is actually—this series is actually—*not* from cuneiform sources; it is actually an esoteric series of texts that were *alluded* to be from such sources and from the

Eastern Orient. It's actually—the *"Book of Dzyan"*—it's actually starting to achieve some interest again in some of the rising "New Thought" that's being put out there.

But, it's a description of, basically, what we've already been dealing with at a systemological or an Anunnaki level at the higher level of understanding—this is how it was relayed in the Theosophical Schools about 150 years ago. And the first part consists of—surprise, surprise—Seven Tablets describing cosmic evolution and creation, which are described in Madame Blavatsky's *"Secret Doctrine"*—*Volume One* being *"Cosmogenesis."*

And then there's Twelve Tablets that compose the second part, which regards Human origins—and what's referred to as *"Anthropogenesis."* And, basically, this is included to show parallels—esoteric developments—from a different stream, but that kinda run parallel with the work of the systemology behind not only the Gatework, but the Anunnaki fragmentation and programming of the Human Condition.

While this may have been an inspirational source to many—and one of the few points of reference that we had during the early developments of the systemology of this work, *from* the Grade-II level, we of course know that the Mardukite Systemology is a far more superior method for accessing the same qualities of information.

In "Tablet-E," I just include some basic information concerning *eclipses* and the "astrology" and the manner in which that was—the significance that that had; obviously in Babylon, we have the first "astronomers"—the actual scientific charting and the mathematics that involves the calculation of astronomy, prediction of eclipses, the designation of the zodiac, the significance of the signs of the zodiac, the signs of the zodiac as Sun Signs and Moon Signs—all that is in "Tablet-E."

And then "Tablet-F"—this is actually the *"Tablet of Fifty*

Names"—and this is, essentially, the *last* portion of the *Enuma Eliš*, but because again, we're sorting these in a catalogue just based on their tablet designation as a title, this is actually given first in sequence here. And so, we have the *"Tablet of Fifty Names,"* where by the end of the *Enuma Eliš*, Marduk assumes all of the properties and powers and attributes and correspondences that were previously divided amongst all these Gates and figures and so forth.

Now, in "Tablet-G" series, you have *"The Book of Generations"* and the "birth" of Man. So, of course, we have the tablets concerning the creation and disposal of Man; which includes the Adamu, the actual development of the worker class as the Adamu; Adapa, which was the—we brought up before in a previous lecture—being the direct descendant of Enki and being treated as the "Wise One," given special schooling as a special lineage; and then the Deluge tablets, which essentially describe the efforts of Enki and Marduk to make certain that Human civilization—that they have spent so much time working to develop and cultivate on the planet Earth—was able to sustain itself as "genetic vehicles."

And then, in "Tablet-H" we have *"The Book of Headaches and Demonologie"*—and these specific tablets, we start to deal with the *"Surpu Tablets,"* some elements of the *"Maqlu Tablets"*—and basically later derived superstitions and so forth that were connected to the various currents and incidents of life as they applied; and of course, being treated—at a certain extent—as "forces" of the "gods," different "intelligences" of the "gods" or the "Wills" of the "gods"—given their own personas, personalities, identities.

A lot of individuals have emphasized the "demonologie" of Mesopotamia and unfortunately so; it's such a miniscule element of the way in which the worldview is interpreted—it's sad that it's what is given most of the interest.

The "Tablet-I" series is mainly concerned with just giving a brief preview—it was the *"Book of Inform"* originally—that was used as a "cypher lexicon" originally, to interpret or transcribe some basic terms and words in the language. It's hardly a complete dictionary by any means; it's just meant to be used as reference and as a guide point.

And then "Tablet J"—we start dealing with the "Yezidic" tribe and the "Yezidic" books of the esoteric. And the Yezidic individuals are—they're basically their own culture and race, which they have a distinct genealogy and a completely separate bloodline from the remaining population or the surrounding populations in the Ancient Near East.

There's a lot of lore and such that's been connected to that —it's been used not only in interpretations of "Kabbalistic" and Judeo-Christian "magic," but other forms of –well, the Left-Hand Path unfortunately, and other permutations— which, if you look at it, again, kind of like "Tablet-D," this is just another interpretation of Cosmic Law, the basic formation of the Universes, partitioning—fragmentation—and the consequential development of the Human Condition and its programming and so forth.

Each of the ancient traditions seems to have a *innate* "intuition" about the qualities of these aspects—and they all run pretty synchronous with each other, concerning the development of the Cosmos, or "Cosmology," and the development of the Human Condition. And it's only later [afterward, relatively more recently] that we see more "wild" mythological applications to this, but, in the beginning the key symbolism behind a lot of this is pretty straightforward.

Now, in "Tablet-K" we end up giving, essentially, the complete *"King-Lists"* in addition to the various manners in which kingship descended from heaven and *"The World Order of Enki,"* because, again, we're dealing with the Earthly realm and we're dealing with "Mardukite Systemology"—*or* the Mardukite systematization of the Anunnaki Tradition.

And "Tablet-L," we have "*The Book of The Law*"—and specifically "*The Book of the Law of Marduk*," how it was delivered to Hammurabi, the wisdom of the kings, the transfer of power and "Enlilship" *to* Marduk on Earth, and then various prayers and writings from different kings.

And then, "Tablet-M"—the "Tablet-M0" [*zero*] series—was originally just some basic incantations and popular translations *from* the "*Maqlu*" series. It doesn't really actually replace the translation work that we eventually participated in for the entire "*Maqlu Tablet Series*"—*nine* tablets in all—which is a large ceremonial application that in addition to now appearing translated *in* the [*Complete*] "*Anunnaki Bible*," it originally only appeared in small parts in that.

And finally, when we did "*Maqlu Magic*"—or "*Liber-M*"—I was able to provide a complete translation, with background information and more material; and then we've been able to revise and enhance it even further, and that information has been used to compose the—some of the more recent versions—such as what appears in your Grade-II textbook there; and also, for Mardukite Zuism, a companion pocket hardcover to go along with "*Anunnaki Bible New Standard Zuist Edition*" and "*The Complete Book of Marduk by Nabu*," we also have "*The Maqlu Ritual Book.*"

The "*Maqlu*" is an interesting series of tablets and ceremonial operation. It basically has to do with purging emotional ties, getting rid of the old, being able to shed skin, release, burning in effigy, targets of anything and any kind of discomfort, any kind of emotional reactivity—very interesting work.

For purposes of the "*Necronomicon*" and the "*Anunnaki Bible*"—and its original presentation: "*Liber-N*"—the *Enuma Eliš* was presented as "*The Book of Nemesis*" and so it was given the designation of "Tablet-N." So, it's the "Tablet-N" series in "*The Complete Anunnaki Bible*" or "*Anunnaki Bible*" that provides the *Enuma Eliš* in total.

The "Tablet-O" series—"*The Book of Oracles*" or "*Book of Chaldean Oracles*"—and it's actually attributed to Zoroaster, which is a Persian, a later post-Babylonian Persian originator of the "Zoroastrian Tradition." But this is part of the—the "Tablet-O" series are part of the origins of "Hermetic Tradition" and the Hermetic sciences and Hermetic philosophy that became the traditional "magic" that would be explored, for example, in Grade-I.

"Tablet-P" is "*The Book of Prayers*"—Anunnaki liturgy examples, some litanies, prayers, different hymns; some of the stuff that we were able to derive from ancient tablets. For the purposes of *modern* Mardukite Zuism, we'll be developing a whole—kind of like in line with the books that we have for that, the "*Anunnaki Bible*" and "*Book of Marduk*" and so forth—we'll be a developing a little bit more modernized applications to deliver that for both a priesthood and for priestesses; developing clergy—Mardukite Ministers—and all of that kind of work. But, for the purposes of the [*Complete*] "*Anunnaki Bible*" has a selection of prayers that *could* be used in invocations.

"Tablet-Q" is—this went in... "Liber-9" tended to deal with some of the "darker" aspects, exorcisms, healing and so forth—we see more of that appearing in "Tablet-Q."

"Tablet-R" is kind of a precursor to the material given in "Tablet-S." This is "*The Book of Return or Last Days.*" There are a lot of *prophetic* books and tablets describing various forthcoming downfalls of Babylon, rises and falls of nations—you know, your traditional apocalyptical spiritual writings [*laughs*].

So, you find a bit of that in "Tablet-R"—the "Tablet-R" series—and then that goes right into "Tablet-S"—"*The Book of Sajaha-the-Seer of Babylon*" and "*...Seer of Marduk*"—and who lived during the time of King Nebuchadnezzar II. So, now we're dealing with tablets from the Neo-Babylonian Renaissance period and, you know, about 600 B.C.

And the "Sajaha" series, again, deals with a lot of Hermetic philosophy—it also is a bridge into Systemology, because it's one of the series of "Arcane Tablets" that are dealt with in Grade-III—in *"The Tablets of Destiny"* volume. So... There's also prophetic visions for the downfall of Babylon in ancient times and the rise of a "New Babylon" and so forth—some of the prophetic material that was [*even*] used in the establishment of the *modern* Mardukite Tradition.

So then, the "Tablet-T" series—we come to *"The Book of Nabu-Tutu"*—which, along with "Tablet-O," pretty much is the backbone and foundations of all future Hermetic Philosophy and so forth. In this instance, we're dealing with *"The Book of Nabu,"* which is information or knowledge—which is relayed as a dialogue or a discourse between Nabu and Marduk; and in this instance, Nabu is referred to as "Nabu-Tutu."

And "Tutu" in Sumerian—the Babylonian language—is transferred to *"Tahuti"* in the Egyptian systems, which is essentially the "magical system" of Thoth. And so we see, again, parallels between the two systems. Here we find a relay, though, of just basic instruction and guidelines of how to carry out the Mardukite Tradition—as religion.

This is being given—the dialogue is set up between—speaking from inside a pyramid; while he's imprisoned, according to the Anunnaki Council—or he's, you know, sentenced to a period of imprisonment—which again leads to decline of Babylon and so, Nabu is there to basically get information on how to keep things going and repair things in his absence.

And this is, again, one of those references to points where to the esteem of Babylon—and its ability to freely rise—and the Mardukite Empire, to reach its heights, is repeatedly thwarted and repeatedly being gouged from Enlilite hands or in relation to—I was talking about the constellations and so forth; there were so many times it would be demonstrated—because of how small the Aries constellations was—that it was "not yet time" for Babylon to rise. So, it was constantly under attack; and yet was able to withstand many many *many* generations of succession and development and really was able to reach some incredible pinnacles, *even in spite of all this*, for the ancient world.

Now, towards the end of the [*Complete*] "Anunnaki Bible," we start to deal with more interesting and *colorful*... demonstrations [*laughs*] of the personal life of the Anunnaki—the "Tablet-U"—or "*The Book of the Underworld*"—discusses the marriage of Nergal and Ereshkigal and there is a lot of *activity* present in this. Another being the "*Courtship of Ishtar and Dumuzi.*"

The kind of stories relayed here certainly provide some *interesting*—almost Harlequin Romance type—information. [*Laughs*] Very colorful; very descriptive... and poetic and artistic at the same time; but both of these [*Ishtar and Ereshkigal*] being very powerful female figures and definitely demonstrate that, in terms of choosing their consorts the establishment of "marital rights" and the demands on such.

In "Tablet-V," we're looking at "*The Book of Variations and Fluctuations*"—one of the first, of course, being the "*Usurpation of Anu.*" And this is actually a—it descends from actually a Hittite text of cuneiform—where Anu is actually usurping the position of "Alalu," and so you see Alalu being this original "King of Heaven." And because of improper rule—the people, basically, revolting against him—and due to plight of their civilization, Alalu is cast out and sent down—he's the first of the Anunnaki to be sent down *to* planet Earth and sentenced here.

And so here, you actually see—you know, you read between the lines now, from a Grade-III and above; because we actually deal with this more at the "Wizard Levels" of *upper-grade* Systemology—but Earth, very first and foremost, in these tablets, is being treated as a "Prison Planet."

It's where Alalu is being sent and exiled from the "Abode Above," and then in time, everybody begins coming down here and kinda making a thing of it.

There's references—some of you have used the Sitchinesque references to "Nibiru" and a *planet* on the verge of collapse —but regardless of how you look at it: we're looking at a previous existence—or a previous "higher" universe, or another realm of "Being"—that is essentially "collapsing" or is, you know, reached the point now where it's created a secondary universe or a lower level of existence in which to send people as penalties or to imprison.

The *Erra Epos*—the Nergal attacks on Babylon; the "Tower of Babel" incident—and various points when Babylon is attacked, "variations" in its control, are also given in the "Tablet-V" series.

And then, "Tablet-W" is actually one-to-one with "Liber-W"—and this is the original text for "*The Book of Marduk by Nabu.*" Now, this has been expanded for the pocket edition to include other information as a reference—as a pocket reference. But, the original complete text for "*The Book of Marduk by Nabu*" was essentially incorporated into the [*Complete*] "Anunnaki Bible" as the "Tablet-W" series.

Now, in "Tablet-X" we're dealing with "*The Book of Crossings and Ilu Star-Gates*" and this is the point when we're introducing the "Star-Gates"—the structure of the Universe and the positions of the Anunnaki and the way it's been systematized for both "higher" spiritual purposes and also for ritual "religious" ceremonial practices.

And it is from this type of material—which became standardized relatively more recently, especially during the age of Nebuchadnezzar II—that we see the Judeo-Christian "Semitic" *Kabbalah* being developed from.

And then in conjunction with that, to further the concept of "ceremonial notes," we have "Tablet-Y," which includes just the basic structure of what we were referring to before as the "Incantation of Eridu" and the setup of what I was talking about in terms of anchor points and sacred space and directing Self and Will—all that is basically summarized for that purpose.

We're just treating this at a ritualistic—almost rising just above into the "Hermetic" level from the Grade-I understandings; and then we'll be taking all this to an even higher level, once we get into Grade-III "Mardukite Systemology," but you can see all the basic seeds for it being planted already here within these texts.

It's just simply (that), once we reach Grade-III, we're looking at some of the basic materials with a much higher level of understanding—and then moving *beyond* the semantics and the idea of a strict regimen of "religious" connotations and so forth, for this existence, and the material universe, and breaking into more spiritual and "metahuman" existences and levels of *thought* and command as *Spirit* and so forth, which is what we get up to in upper-levels; *that's* the "exploration."

I mean... all of the "ledges" are scaled and developed—the Grades for them—are scaled and developed in such a way that all of this becomes easily reachable as we move along; as almost a "common sense" natural progression of the information—as if this was just, you know, the natural way of things.

In doing so, we're never pitting someone up against something that's too high a gradient or too far out of reach. I know, at the Mardukite Master Course level, I allude to, for example—because it's the work we're doing now; *this* has all been set down and printed—but the work we are doing now for these other Grades is still taking place and it's following along the same gradients up to higher and higher levels past what we are doing, for example, in the Grade-II work here—and then in Grade-III. And it's just a natural evolution of the understanding.

Finally, for the *"Anunnaki Bible,"* we now have all the Zoroastrian tablets—concerning the litanies and sacrifices and hymns and incantations and prayers and such—as an example, because it was a Persian extension of the same Ancient Near East work that we've been covering—all that appears as "Tablet-Z." It's really just there as a reference point.

That was one of the purposes of establishing this library of materials for the Mardukite Chamberlains is—it was *us* developing our own "Research Library" *of* materials *as* we went along, so that we have this for posterity; we could make comparisons—everything of which could be still self-contained *within* the "Mardukite Core."

And that's one of the reasons that the *"Necronomicon: The Complete Anunnaki Legacy"*—this edition that we've been able to put out now for 2020, which contains materials from over *fifteen* different discourses or release or books from over a decade—this is, I mean, this is essentially the *entire* library that the "Mardukite Chamberlains" were putting together during its development.

And from this we were even able to launch forth into a more practical *modernized* application of "Mardukite Zuism"—in terms of applying this to, you know, the "New Age" contemporary "Neopagan" realm that we've been occupying, in which we are not unfamiliar with, when we look at the background in Druidism and practical magic and the Ritual Tech and all of that; but of which it is really only the efforts of the Mardukite Chamberlains since 2008 and 2009, that we've been basically pushing forth to find our place—to have a place for "Mesopotamian Neopaganism" and in the light of the fact that *every other* culture and *every other* example and system *since this* has been pretty much dug up and brought out for some kind of "New Age" revival.

That information behind us—and of course, I just have kind of burned through what is relayed as 500—600—pages worth of material there in about 20-30 minutes; but with that behind us and the introduction present—that we spent the last couple days working on—we'll be able to easily get through the last half of the Grade-II material early next week, be able to bridge it smoothly into Grade-III material with "*The Tablets of Destiny*" and complete our Mardukite Master Course on *all three* "Master Levels" of material.

From the "Route of Magic and Mysticism" and "Druidry and the Dragon Legacy"—which we've been able to relay over this last week and I know it's been a very intensive week of instruction, presentations, these recorded lectures—*and also additional processing that have been working on other levels here this week.*

But we've been able to get through all of that; we've been able to introduce Grade-II "Mardukite Zuism"; we've been able to introduce the cuneiform tablets—the structure of Mesopotamia and the Anunnaki pantheon—and go through the catalogue of Tablets that we use as a reference point within the Grade-II Mardukite Chamberlains "Core"; and this will easily progress.

As we go further, we'll go into the *Enuma Eliš* and we'll get into the Systemology and structure of the "Standard Model" for Grade-III—which, integrates this knowledge directly, for our Systemology and the whole backbone of our Systemology.

[*So, with all this in the bag—and just really only a couple more day of instruction coming up next week—I'd like to wish everybody a nice safe and sane weekend and we will meet right back here on Monday to get through the rest of this material.*]

: LECTURE 33—NECRONOMICON REVELATIONS :
(September 28, 2020)

[*Good morning. It's now the thirty-third lecture of the Mardukite Master Course. This is for the morning lectures of September 28, 2020—and we're dealing with Grade-II material; a continuation from last week. Today, we'll be transitioning from Grade-II into Grade-III, and we'll be able to wrap up the Mardukite Master Course in the next couple days.*]

Although the term comes up—the title comes up—frequently throughout our discussions of "magic," the presentation of it particularly with our Grade-II material... it just wouldn't be a *Mardukite* Master Course [*laughs*], if we didn't actually spend some time discussing the subject of the *Necronomicon*.

Now, it's curious because I honestly haven't really haven't discussed this subject as verbally for quite a few years, now. Most of the people I've been working with for the last several years [*laughs*] have either already heard or read almost everything I pretty much have to say [*laughs*] regarding the "Necronomicon." And although it's, you know, we used it as a title to represent, for example, the original presentations of the Mardukite Chamberlains work and the "Mardukite Core," it was really not until the completion of the historical work—the presentation of the tablets, the background for that—that I began to delve, specifically, back to the semantic applications of "Necronomicon."

My involvement with it—as an application; as a philosophical example of Mesopotamian mysticism and "magic"—really began back in the 1990's; and that's pretty evident with the "Merlyn Stone" material and particularly everything that's regarding that subject in "*The Great Magickal Arcanum*," which was developed prior to the inception of Mardukite

Chamberlains and the Mardukite research material in 2008 —it prompted all that, really, to get going.

And at the time *"Arcanum"* was published by "Mardukite Truth Seeker Press"—so, it was the first publication, and the only publication, for nearly a year, to be developed under the Mardukite "banner." And what we found was that a lot of individuals were either understanding or coming into this information based on the "Ancient Aliens" paradigm— which is popularized by the work of Zecharia Sitchin and then, of course, now, the television programs that have been inspired from that—and then of course, the "Simon Necronomicon." These were the main two ways in which individuals had *any* background in the nomenclature and the semantics and the paradigm *of* for example, the Anunnaki or Mesopotamia in general.

This was readily observed and easily worked with because, for example, as "Merlyn Stone" working in the 1990's, I had already put a lot of emphasis, kinda behind the scenes and with the groups I was working with—on the "Necronomicon." Not necessarily its use verbatim, because I had already started piecing together the various elements of where it was lacking, in regards to a true revival of Mesopotamian Neopaganism back in the 1990's; it just wasn't something I was delivering yet. And that would take another ten years of development—kind of on the back-burner—while I was working on other things; working on other "Druid" projects and then the "Elven" project and *"Arcanum."*

But it was all kind of leading toward a certain point and at the time that I had launched the Mardukites, one of the underground figures that I was friends with, was just starting up their own publishing company, and they had previously publishing under various names—had run some underground organizations—and bringing in a new face to the internet age and what was considered "Web 2.0" at the time. And her name was Tracy Twyman—she's since *crossed beyond* the work of this dimension.

And she knew Peter Levenda, she knew Nicholas de Vere—she knew a lot of figures that were involved with this underground chain of Mesopotamian mysticism. And so, she ended up publishing—by arrangement with me—the original [*commercial*] presentation of our "*Liber-N*," as the "Necronomicon," which was a previously a handmade "Lapis Edition."

I was, in 2009, hand-making all of the books. So, the original presentations—all of them handmade and hand-numbered, prior to development of the "*Anunnaki Bible*." But these were mainly—although they mention the "Necronomicon" and that certain elements of Mesopotamian lore, as was being relayed, may have appeared in there and some small connections—I wasn't really pushing, you know, the actual examination of all these cross-points at that time; it wasn't something...

I was trying to examine it from a purely Mesopotamian perspective—as we've pretty much been doing so far in Grade-II—and rather than trying to really emphasize, you know, the application of the "Simon" work. All of those that were coming into the *fray* from that—using that as their entry point—were *already* familiar with the Simon work; that didn't need any prompting by me. They had already had that; were familiar with the concepts, the Gates, the sequence of the "Ladder of Lights" and some basic background of the "*Simonian*" version of, for example, the *Maqlu* or the *Enuma Eliš*—the Tablets of Creation.

That didn't require any prompting by me, I was simply trying to *use* that as a representation of what this was, because *that* was actually very inspirational to *me* in the 1990's. There really weren't any other presentations of this kind of work at that time—and there's still very few other representations of the caliber, and the caliber that *we're* doing, that treat this level of Mesopotamian Neopaganism and information.

The work of "*Necronomicon: The Anunnaki Bible*" was meant to be capped off, actually, with "Liber-9" originally. And "Liber-9" was presented also as "*Nine Gates of the Kingdom of Shadows.*" It's actually only the "Tablet" (text) forms that appeared in "Liber-9."

There was a lot of weird stuff going on at the time, during the early years of the Mardukite operations. I was having to, kind of, work around not only the politics of the work we were doing but also the, I guess, "challenges" of pursuing this work *full time.*

I've been now working with the Mardukite Research Organization, Mardukite Chamberlains, the Council of Nabu, the Mardukite Truth Seeker Press—which is now The Joshua Free Imprint—the establishment years ago of a study group or social network called "Moroii ad Vitam," which was for Alumni *prior to* the establishment of not only the Mardukite Academy, but the Systemology Society.

So, now the founding of all this was midsummer 2008—but by a year later, the Summer Solstice of 2009, I was doing this *full time.* So, I've been doing this *full time* in the underground—only recently been working to develop a more "mainstream" presence, now that we've been able to solidify the work. I've been mostly concerned with *the work* itself for the past decade—for example, solidifying what we're delivering as the Mardukite Master Course here.

Unfortunately the work for "Liber-9" ended up being cut short, and rather than getting right back to *that* project—because it was meant to be a bridge to, essentially, Systemology. I was starting to work on Systemology back in 2008 and just, kind of, was waiting—once I could get enough researchers involved, a network of discussion, experimentation and development. I was waiting to get enough involved before unleashing that.

I mean, the concept behind [*Systemology*] is present in virtually all of introductory material and the prefaces [*to the original "Anunnaki Bible"*] and so forth, as far as I was where I was intending on taking all this.

But, unfortunately "*Liber-9*" *didn't* complete the picture I was trying to relay at the time. And when I eventually—once actually having to move across the country, several thousand miles, multiple times in just a few months.

When I was finally able to get back into the work of what was—what had been basically been piling up to do—what was considered "Year-2" work was already in demand; and that ended up being "*Liber-50*"—"*Sumerian Religion*" or "*Gates of the Necronomicon*" or information concerning the Sumerian Anunnaki directly that we were talking about last week. And then "*The Book of Marduk by Nabu.*"

And this was, I mean, I had already put so many things in motion; and while we were still kind of backed up on where we were trying to take things at the time, there was already a need to continue the work—there were others involved aside from just me [*laughs*] and there was a schedule needing to be maintained in order to develop the work and everything that we were doing.

So, by the time—it took several months after completing that work for me to get back to where things were actually supposed to be headed at the end of "*Liber-9*." And it actually kind of worked out for the best—everything, you know, has its own reasons—in delivering things to the point we've got to now. Because "*Sumerian Religion*"—the "*Liber-50*" material—really helped in bringing *to life* any kind of personal relationship or affinity or being able to really establish a *connection* with the Anunnaki paradigm; especially because this is not something that is treated other than, for example, the "Simon Necronomicon."

This was not a paradigm that was being treated regardless of someone's background in various ritual magic traditions that are being revived in the New Age—kind of like what we were discussing in Grade-I.

So, the "*Liber-9*" material was later re-released along with "*Necronomicon Revelations*," which is "*Liber-R*"—and we finally did a combined edition that was called "*Novem Portis.*" And it was meant to kind of have the same—following in the tradition of the pseudoepigrapha that was iconic and archetypal and classic in terms of *consciousness* and "pop-culture" and so forth—in regards to our work—the "Delomelanicon" or "Nine Gates of the Kingdom of Shadows" and "Novem Portis."

These all seemed very much integrated occult themes. And at Grade-II, while we were basically capping off the work of the Mardukite Chamberlains—the original research and development work—we were still looking at, really, an extension, or a Hermetic application of the same applications that would be treated more popularly in today's society—like for example, Grade-I; just the more popular aspects of metaphysics and "magical traditions" and so forth.

So, here again, we were dealing with another iconic presentation of a "legendary book"—you know, a "dangerous, valuable, rare legendary book of forbidden secrets" or, in the case of "*Novem Portis*," having been written by the "Devil" himself as the "Delomelanicon" and then rewritten as "Nine Gates of the Kingdom of Shadows" and so forth.

There were a lot of themes attached to that, that we were finding interesting applications of—because, back in 2009 and 2010, we were still treating the Mardukite work—not as Zuism, not as Systemology, but as an extension of, for example, what we've treated as Grade-I in the Mardukite Master Course. And so, we were still using a lot of these type of themes that had a lot to do with "mysticism" and the dark culture of that—the kind of "shadow side" or "underground" of the "New Age Mystery Traditions."

It was just... kind of a *different* time; not only in the development of the Mardukites, but also in relation to "world consciousness" at that time, the establishment of social networking on the internet, and the development of all these groups and niches—because, when we're talking about "Nine Gates of the Kingdom of Shadows" or "Novem Portis" or we're talking about the "Necronomicon"—even when we're talking about Mesopotamia and the Anunnaki—we're actually talking about some pretty unique niches of these, what has otherwise been overshadowed by other more colorful fanciful or popularized, or with a more more visible tradition.

So, with the rise of the internet, it actually allowed for a lot of different networking concerning those that were *really* only occupying these specific recesses or alleyways of the "New Age" underground.

Now, the "Simon" book—it's very interesting, it's been very useful for our purposes—it's been kind of a landmark for not only the Lovecraftian tradition, but also it's become kind of iconic for a representation of Mesopotamia and its applications to neopaganism. Up until the presentations of the "Mardukite Core"—and it's not to replace; I don't know that we'll ever reach the point that our work is as widespread as the "Simon" book, which has already sold over a million copies and who knows how many secondhand readerships it's got.

It's not about competition—it's simply that our work has been an extension of many of the concepts and allusions that have been presented within the themes that... we're very, I mean in terms of the time period that it was developed—the available research at the time—really it's an incredible attempt at bringing consciousness and opening up the doorway to the Anunnaki paradigm. And it is for that reason that it primarily existed—and that reason it was developed and released and became a turning point, in 1977, towards a "New Age."

We've been in a completely different world since then—in both mystical and technological and all kinds of things in terms of consciousness. Don't forget, 1977—we talked about the *"Shannara"* series, when I was discussing the "Elves" and such, that was first launched in 1977 with *"The Sword of Shannara."* You had *"Star Wars"* in 1977. You had all of this stuff shifting. It's also interesting to note that the first book by Sitchin—*"The Twelfth Planet"*—and the "Simon Necronomicon" both emerged around the same time.

And so, there's a shift in consciousness taking place; without which, I don't know that we would *even* have the "Mardukite Tradition" and "New Babylon Rising" and the work that we've been doing—that the Mardukite Master Course is representative of.

I did actually give details regarding my personal work—my personal explorations—the discoveries concerning the underground occult tradition, whether it be Aleister Crowley, Kenneth Grant, the Typhonian materials; things that tied in both with the "Necronomicon" as it was, at that time, only real known as for the "Simon" edition, and "Mesopotamia."

One of the key points—one of the main "revelations" or why *"Necronomicon Revelations"* was originally released this way—is that the piercing of the veil, concerning the Seven Gates, was basically meant to demonstrate what we do with the Standard Model and the higher realizations of this understanding in Grade-III; but it was leading to the "Infinity of Nothingness" and this was essentially the points we were trying to get back to.

I picked this up, originally, you'll notice—if you notice—when we were talking about the sequence of material that I was telling you "Liber-9" was cut off with just the tablet material that was later incorporated into the [Complete] "Anunnaki Bible." And then, rather than wrapping up—what I was assuming to be the Grade at that time; we had only originally planned on doing that many pieces of work for the main textbook and then moving on to other things. That research period, though, ended up extended several more years, to develop now what is the Grade-II textbook, "*Necronomicon: The Complete Anunnaki Legacy*"—this 2020 Master Edition hardcover that we now have.

You will notice that in "*Liber-50*"—concerning the Sumerian Anunnaki, "*Sumerian Religion*" and such—that I was actually already in that "mind-set" when I started presenting the "roll-call" or the sequence or the background mythology and mysticism of the Anunnaki; because I (had) started off talking about "Abzu" and "Nothingness" and the background reality behind the ALL and such; and this was entirely relevant and coherent to the work that was being done at the time—but that was where I was already at and what I was working with at the time; piercing these veils and seeing that.

The other great revelations behind it, which isn't really as strictly or blatantly pointed out concerning the work of, for example, the "Simon Necronomicon" or how we had been treating the "Gate-work" up until that point, is that—what I was explaining, I believe, in one of the Grade-I lectures now —these "Seven Gates" were being treated still from a Grade-I point-of-view.

So, we were treating—based on the available materials at the time, prior to completing the Mardukite Chamberlains work and then moving on to Grade-III—prior to that, we ourselves, and most of the people—because this was not just a single effort by me; yes, I did all the writing and publishing and organization of the structure and the underground society at the time—but, we still had a lot of individuals who were working with this material all around the globe that were participating and discussions and such *about* the work.

And it became clear that this was still all being treated at "ceremonial magic" level; that the "Simon Necronomicon" was, kind of, something that was *so ingrained* now *in* consciousness—and its connections, for example, if you were to apply the same paradigm and overlap it on the other methods of "planetary magick" and "ceremonial magic" and "grimoire magic" and all of this stuff that we treat in Grade-I.

The fact that it was *still* being treated that way *meant* we were working through *seven veils* or *seven gates* still at the *first* level. So, this was kind of... I mean, we were kinda like, "Whoa!" That means there's like *fifty gates* now—and then suddenly some other things began making more sense, since this number *Fifty* was showing up so much more.

It was actually—and this is how we've structured and graded the Mardukite Master Course, and honestly, even continuing on into the later Grades now—of Systemology. Because, we had a Grade-I understanding at the *lunar level* and then using that to uncover or treat Mesopotamia—or what we now treat as Grade-II—it was discovered that, "Well, you can *treat* Mesopotamia from a Grade-I level, but that's as far as you're getting."

And then, when it was done successfully—and if you were actually to go through all that, because that's inherently what we're doing with the Mardukite Master Course; that's why we're structuring it this way—you would suddenly start to realize these new *higher* level understanding; which is like the "Hermetic Mysteries," the stuff dealt with in the "Tablet-O" and the "Tablet-T" series and so on, "Tablet-S" and all of those types of—the "Arcane Tablets"—as they appear in the "Anunnaki Bible" and your Grade-II textbook. And then as their applied, again, to *higher* Systemological understanding in Grade-III—and that basically prompting higher levels.

We've basically structured this—and are delivering it—in the same method that's been developed, where the Master understanding of Grade-I and its application to Mesopotamia led to the realizations that allowed for a Master understanding of Grade-II. *That* Master level understanding *is* the bridge to Grade-III material, which I presented only just a year ago—a little over a year ago—as *"The Tablets of Destiny."*

In that, there is your "progression" and it's really—it can't be rushed and it can't be cheated; it can't be side-stepped. An individual can continue going on and reading and understanding and experiencing life however they choose. They can read the later Grade work, they can study, they can go and have all these...

Still, unless they've reached a new ledge of understanding—a ledge of Knowingness, or a knowledge, the True Knowledge that is inherent behind all of this—it is *still* going to be treated at lower levels; lower levels of understanding and never anything further.

This is what we discovered with the *Gates*; we discovered essentially that the Gate-work as it was being treated, was still only going to keep one contained within the *lunar level* of understanding; that the deeper "Hermetic" mysteries that the Second Grade or the Second Gate or "Level-2" work and so forth—what *it* represents is essentially the "Sphere of Mercury" and the "Nabu Gate."

That's only really *tapped* by getting into the heart *of* Mesopotamia as we've been discussing it and the tablets of the "Anunnaki Bible" as they are found from a complete perspective and from within the Mesopotamian paradigm in contrast to, for example, the "Simon Necronomicon," which really—if we were looking at it in strictly the way we are grading the *Pathway to Self-Honesty* or these *Gateways to Infinity* and demonstrating them in the Mardukite Master Course—the "Simon Necronomicon" would still, for all intents and purposes, be a Grade-I application.

There's nothing wrong with that; and there's nothing wrong with being able to go back to it and look at it later and see these other elements within it, because you've already seen the way they're laid out, for example, within *our* "*Necronomicon: The Complete Anunnaki Legacy*" or the way that the tablets are laid out in any of its editions as "*Necronomicon: The Anunnaki Bible.*"

As a mentor, or as a Master Instructor—you know, which is what we're kind of gearing more of these lectures towards, as opposed to general education or audiobook read-alongs of the materials—the "Simon Necronomicon" has been... It can't be compared to in regards to the pop-culture or mainstream tie-in or entry-point that you might have with a Seeker in bringing them to a Grade-II interest; if that's the only real background that they have regarding these kind of topics, you know?

As long as, again, just like we're kinda keeping out a watch for those we are mentoring or apprenticing at your Wizard Schools and Magic Schools and such—it's just making sure they don't get too trapped into the semantics or the paradigms or the understandings that are really just symbolic additions that are put in place to help give different things a framework; such as when you find any correlations or applications to the fantasy-gothic horror of, for example, H.P. Lovecraft.

It is from within those texts—the Lovecraftian "Cthulhu" Mythos—that we first really see this now popular term "Necronomicon" appear in literature. As a practical application, the "Lovecraftian" traditions, some of the Typhonian Tradition, most of the things that have come before—all of the Grade-I traditions—all of them were actually meant to be, essentially, *trappings* to continue to hold an individual down at this, kind of, material universe level of understanding and considerations as a point-of-view. We talked about some of that in the Grade-I lectures.

In Grade-II, the idea being that there is an Infinity of Gateways; and therefore when treated at only a Grade-I level of understanding—although you're working in Grade-II at this point, with the materials—but without having flattened or resolved the type of work that we discussed in Grade-I; what ends up happening is that an individual starts *spiraling in* to that, and keeps applying that *same* concept to each higher and higher level, which doesn't end up actually end up being a higher and higher level, but a lower and lower level.

Lower and lower levels of consideration—each one opening into *one more* and *one more* and *one more*. It's essentially a "puzzle box" that an individual gets lost into; and *there* being the *trapping* at the *entry* into Grade-II; because, we're either accessing the Gate that's *actually* Grade-II and arriving at new levels of realization concerning, for example, the Hermetic philosophies and such—and which, they themselves are not perfect.

But, when someone begins to just look at it from, for example, the "Left-Hand Path," the "Cthulhu Mythos"—a lot of these "darksider" traditions that have been popularized *around* the "Necronomicon" and anything regarding "Mesopotamia"—these are all, basically, "artificial veils."

What it's meant to do is focus an individual's attention on a perpetual Mystery—and the Mystery becomes the "Darkness"; what is actually, you know: when one *thinks* they have reached the "Infinity of Nothingness" and one *thinks* they have actually peeled back all of the layers, rather than *arrive* at the Second Gate, they are given the illusion that they have arrived at the "Infinity of Nothingness" which is actually *not* the "Infinity of Nothingness," but a *substitution* for that *within still* the First Circle or First Sphere of Existence, which *is* essentially the "Perpetual Mystery."

And it is the Perpetual Mystery—the *failure* to actually reach a state of Knowingness as Beingness and instead be compulsively looking for the *next* thing to *know* (or *be*) to open the *next* "Gate"; the *next*... just *one more bit* of information will get you there; just *one more* classification of the sciences; just *one more* division of the nucleus—this concept of that: if we just work at this Physical Universe, or this Grade-I level of understanding just enough, that we'll somehow be able to pierce to Grade-II with it... It doesn't get there; it really doesn't.

That's part of the—unfortunately what is inherently implanted in the Mind-Systems of the Human Condition, where one is essentially *compelled to know*—to *know*, to *learn*, to *find*, to *discover*... And there's nothing wrong with that *except* that what is being is discovered is simply these "game" aspects where an individual has created things and then hidden them from view and so later they can be found—and all these, kind of, weird parameters that we deal with more at Grade-III and so forth.

But, yeah... It's one of those—the "great" Necronomicon Revelation that we discovered was: yes, it represents what Grade-II *should be*, but unfortunately what the previous treatments—prior to the "Mardukite Core"; the work of the Mardukite Chamberlains—the previous treatments of this lore was still keeping people trapped—initiates and Seekers; no matter how many degrees and levels they had separated this Grade-I knowledge into [*laughs*], you know, for their "schools" and "societies"—it was still keeping them trapped within that.

And as a result of that, the work was not really getting anyone any farther; and of course, any further work, which *we did* with the "Mardukite Core" and what we treat as Grade-II and the Mardukite Master Course—to get any further required almost a ten-year dedication in an underground systematic treatment into what would become this Grade-II material.

By using it—by treating it from the Grade-II perspective, with the Mesopotamian paradigm as we've described it—there's no fear of your Seekers running into the *trappings* that this can lead to *if* not brought to that higher level of realization; and that's why for "Instructor" purposes, for the treatment, we could just as easily capped things off with Grade-II and been like, "Okay, here's all this background magical information and here's all the Mesopotamian information and there you have it, now you've got your Magic School."

But, we had to shoot one higher, you know, into Grade-III, just to make certain that we have a Master level of understanding—and that you can duplicate the type of work that we've actually done here at the Mardukite Academy or at the Mardukite Offices in your individual groups and training and schools.

: LECTURE 34—THE MARDUKITE CORE :
(September 28, 2020)

When we're talking about Grade-II for the Mardukite Master Course—when we're talking about Grade-II for the Mardukite Chamberlains work—Grade-II is the basis of Mardukite Zuism and Mardukite Systemology; we're talking about the "Mardukite Core." Prior to being treated as your Grade-II textbook, "*Necronomicon: The Complete Anunnaki Legacy*," this was called the "Mardukite Core."

It had a particular structure, the "Liber" designations that we've given, the "Tablet" catalog that we've discussed as "The Anunnaki Bible"—all of this was systematized and structured to establish a Research & Discovery Library for all future work regarding the Mardukite umbrella of organizations.

So, in order to establish a standard, we've included the curriculum outline for Grade-II materials—it is the appendix for the Mardukite Master Edition of "*Necronomicon: The Complete Anunnaki Legacy*." It's also in your "*Instructor's Manual*." And this just runs through not only a basic outline of the materials that appear in the "Anunnaki Bible," but also the Discussion Questions that we can actually use as a Grade Review—again, just to make sure we have a certain standard when we speak about a Master-level understanding and Instructor-level duplication of the Mardukite Master Course.

Up until the new standardization and public representation of "Mardukite Zuism," the basic structure of the "Mardukite Core"—the original structure and outline and its review questions—were actually what was used in the last decade, in the underground, in order to *certify* what we considered our "Mardukite Ministers."

In the original 2009 "Introduction to Mardukite Studies," we deal with a few key concepts—and again, this is where I say, there is a direct line between my efforts with the Mardukite Chamberlains *and* the Systemology that I wanted to develop from it.

So, we talk about experience and reality—and that what most people have referred to as "conditioning" and a lot of "behavioral psychology" and what a lot of other physical sciences treat in terms of the Human Condition—is really going back to the idea that *beliefs* and *thoughts* are filtering the Reality Experience; that these—the fragmentation, the imprinting, all of this experiential programming—this affects experience. And this is one of the first things we point out to an individual when they're about to study the Grade-II material.

We don't want Grade-II being treated as Grade-I—and so, we're introducing, essentially, a *higher* level of thought in the application of the organization of systems, the Human Condition, the understanding of what the Ancient Mystery School was actually representing, but also its downfall.

In the last lecture, when I talked about the Ancient Mystery School, I'm talking about, basically, the inception of all this and where it streamed off—became the entrapping of the "mystical" systems. So, just as "magic" has its own levels and degrees of limitations or *trappings* or pitfalls—and we've discussed that in Grade-I—this is where the Grade-II, for example, that's where the trapping of Grade-II come in.

And really, each one is meant to have its own level of gravity so that you're not just—this isn't just like jumping up a flight of steps. Each one of these rungs—on the Ladder—each one of these tiers requires a specific amount of inertia to get to the next point. It's really better represented in the "ziggurat" structures of ancient Mesopotamia; because you see these large tiers, and yes there is a stairway to ascend them, but each tier—the *stairway* is the gradient pathway of the Self, taking each step within reach to get up to what becomes actual tiers. In between—there's really nothing going on in between; it's about getting to the next tier, so-to-speak.

I'm really not implying that—to rush through the Grades—and that that's the goal. It's that there's two aspects to this: the way in which the individual is actually traveling up the *stairway* and then what they are actually traveling *to*. The "gradients" are steeper; they're actually tiers.

When we talk about *beliefs* and "Ancient History"—this idea of monotheism. Well, you know, to have monotheism, it really requires to have had a multiplicity of gods to begin with. And so, that's one of the aspects that's kind of blotted out of our modern understanding of spirituality or "religion" is that: this development of monotheism, as we observe it today, it's all "One God." And usually they're not even referring to the "Source" or "Infinity."

Most individuals have some kind of conception of which Anu is a good—if you're looking for that *older, wise-looking, bearded, Kingly,* sitting on a throne in a "cloud palace," then Anu is actually the archetype of that. And so that's what's been imprinted in [*laughs*] most individuals regarding the concept of "God"—and however they've interpreted it; whatever name they've given to that—but that's what the source of *that* imprinting really is.

When we're treating the traditions and religion as it extended from ancient Mesopotamia—for example, the Judeo-Christian traditions—we find that the concept of what we discussed before about Enlil and Enki, that each tradition ends up observing one *or* the other as the "Father God" or the one that's prayed to.

For example, in the Mardukite Babylonian Tradition, the succession is essentially: Anu, Enki, Marduk, Nabu—and this is specific to the Babylonian Tradition; this isn't Sumerian, this is specific to the Mardukite Babylonian Tradition.

So, in the more "outer"—because again, Babylon... the only time we're treating Babylon properly is *within* the Mardukite Tradition—which has been outlined for you throughout Grade-II materials—and other than that, what you know of Babylon, what you know of Egypt, what you know of the Anunnaki or their representations in these other paradigms —how they refer to them—really goes back to the Judeo-Christian system and the "Old Testament" system.

It basically refers to "Yahweh" or "Enlil" or "Jehovah" as being the—having all the beneficent qualities; all the ones that, you know, the "one that you pray to"; the one that is the Father of Abraham or God of the Israelites—all of this is being attributed to Enlil. And then as an antithesis to that, we see Enki given the traits of the more "darker"—basically becoming the "Satan" or "Lucifer" to the Judeo-Christian tradition. And so you see that division there.

And the idea of monotheism being, of course, that—to be the *only* "God" requires that there be others there to be the *only* of. And this is one of the things that shifts in—when you're dealing with, you know, the Judeo-Christian tradition in terms of "God," because you don't find this, for example, in Mardukite monaltry; you still see the observance of the other pantheon, but that Marduk has actually taken on all of those attributes, all of those names, abilities, powers, and is *the Way* to Infinity, so to speak.

This is one of the key points though—and it can't be stressed enough—because it is kind of a staple of the Mardukite paradigm, is that: any of these references to the succession of "*Anu-Enki-Marduk-Nabu*," such as you find in the "Simon Necronomicon," are *indicative* of the Babylonian Mardukite worldview—of the Babylonian Mardukite paradigm.

These are not Sumerian; they should not be confused with

Sumerian, which is a culture that existed in the same geography and it actually overlapped, but that culture specifically observed the "Enlilite" lineage; and when we discussed *last week* about the Sumerian Anunnaki, the various divisions of the planetary assignments that *in* the tradition, we're talking about Anu, we're talking about Enlil, we're talking about Nanna and Shammash and Inanna-Ishtar and Nergal—that is the *Sumerian* pantheon from the Sumerian worldview.

Too many times Marduk is being treated, in some respects—even in Zecharia Sitchin's work—he's referred to as a "Sumerian god." In the Necronomicon—"Simon's Necronomicon"—it's referred to many times as a "Sumerian text" or emphasizing a "Sumerian worldview," when it's actually, specifically, Babylonian.

So, these are points that are reiterated several times throughout the "Mardukite Core," but these *are* very key points of what separates the Mardukite tradition—and understanding the *ancient* Mardukite tradition—from other examples of the Anunnaki methodology and paradigm.

So, we've already talked about—and given a review—*last week*, of the Tablet Catalogue given in the "Anunnaki Bible"; so, when we're talking about tablets specific to "*Liber-N*," the discussion that we can have—and the discussion review that we can have regarding that—it just kinda covers all of that inclusively; kind of what we've been talking about at the end of the last week.

For example: "Why are humans initially upgraded by the Anunnaki?" This is discussed in "*The Book of Generations,*" and it alludes to the revolt of the IGIGI "*Watchers*" and as far as doing the work—the physical work—in terms of developing Earth. And when we go back, remember that Alalu—the former "King of the Heavens" or the former "President" of the Heavenly Abode—was cast down here and Earth was originally treated, essentially, as a "prison planet" for the

Anunnaki.

In doing so—there's several references to what's taking place. We know that Alalu was overthrown because of poor leadership and that things had gotten so bad in this *former existence* or other "planet" or "dimension" or "universe," that the people had just had enough; the populations had had enough and new leadership had come into play: which is Anu.

And of course, by the time we've reached the Earth Plane, Anu is the "King of the Gods" and Alalu is this, kinda, backstory that is hardly ever mentioned. But, it's assumed that for whatever purposes that things weren't going so well; and Earth was established originally as a place to put people that were getting in the way of those in this former existence—of basically creating a habitable plane, habitable environment.

At some juncture, basically, Alalu says, "Hey, you know, this is the place to be. You could just settle here; you don't even gotta worry about all the problems going on over there." And so, more and more of the population begins coming to Earth and working on Earth as being set up *as* a habitable environment.

Now, of course, this is the way it's being relayed in the *cuneiform* tablets. We may—for example, this might be about the *Condensation of Universes* as we explore upper-grades of Systemology, or this may have some other implication—but, it does suggest a basic pattern of what happens concerning the development of fragmented universes, with each one being established to put people as a penalty—or as a prison —and then more and more of the population starts to get put there and more and more developments are taking place and you have these "higher minds" coming in and establishing these "expert levels" of *technology* and demonstrating all this stuff that can be done at *this* level of existence; and then making it, again, kinda the "place to be."

I don't want to get too much into that upper-level Systemology for the purposes of the Mardukite Master Course—but, it can... there's many ways in which the Arcane Tablets can, once you have upper-levels of understanding as we develop this and we go through this; and we still have another Grade to work through for the Mardukite Master Course—that these tablets begin to take on different meaning; that you can understand them in different ways. And this is not necessarily one-to-one with the way that, for example, you would be exploring this at an "Academic" level or "scholarly" level at colleges and universities and so forth.

Next question: "What is the purpose of a fragmented polarity-based existence?" [*Laughs*] Of course, we know that this is to create action; to create a game—basically, for purposes of "control" and also to have something to *do*.

I mean, we know that there *is*, outside of all existence, this Infinity of Nothingness, but that: then we reach the point of All, which is contrasting or balancing with the potential creation of Everything; all manifestation—and this dichotomy *right there* is where we have "form" or "not-form," "nothingness" or "everythingness" in existence; it provides for an existence.

The dichotomies and polarities really are only there to create and energy *flow*, to create some *action*—something happening; because, of course, the background static behind all of this, that which is the Infinity of Nothingness *is* exactly *that*. So, to have *anything* that is *otherwise* is to create, for example, some need for polarity or dualism to have something —you know, two "terminals" or two "posts" to have something to act against, to create some kind of *charge* or *flow* of energy between.

The question here: "What is the function of the Gateways of the Babili System?" Well, we know that based on the idea of Marduk representing the Sixth Gate and we look at the Standard Model and higher-level Systemology, we know we're talking about the "Cosmic Ordering"—the systematization and separation of the Spiritual and Physical universes and *Life* taking on Beta-existence on that point, being able to assume a "Mind-System" and so forth.

So, what we find that these Veils or Thresholds or Gateways are essentially the division points or fragmentation points or points of condensation, levels and layers, that separate the "I-AM," the "Self," the "Alpha Spirit" from its own nature—by projecting points-of-views into other layers and considerations; garments, I mean, you could almost, at one point in Beta-existence, consider personalities like "outfits" or "costumes" that are put on—entire personality packages —that are assumed;

And each step of the way, further down the track, as we come down to the lower Gates and to the Earth point, you have this personality-program that is all of the inclinations and restrictions—what an individual is willing to do, not willing to do—all of their responsive mechanisms attached to that identity; none of which is the Self.

When we're talking about Gateways or working back toward Infinity or working back toward a state of Beingness and Knowingness *as* the Alpha Spirit *as* Self, we're talking about moving through these Gateways that have been reflected within these lower, you know: the Star-Gates, the Sumerian Anunnaki, the planetary symbolism—all of this being symbols and icons meant to indicate this Pathway back to Self, and the of course, back to Source.

Next question: "Why does Inanna-Ishtar descend to the Underworld?" I believe we covered that a bit. There's various versions of it, but as one of the stories goes: her consort is killed or drowned and that Marduk is eventually blamed for it—it's the reason why he's imprisoned and why Nabu is speaking to him through the pyramid in the "Tablet-T" series of the "Anunnaki Bible." And so, she's basically going down to rectify this—going down to the Underworld to basically free Dumuzi to come back.

And we see this idea of the "slain and resurrected god" appear multiple times; and given that Inanna-Ishtar is also "Isis," you can see some elements of that—the "Osirian" tradition of Isis and Osiris and the repair of, you know, the "slain god" or the "dead god" and so forth.

When it talks about—the next question: "Explain the spiritual-political purpose of the *Enuma Eliš*." The short version of that, of course, to install Marduk into the pantheon, to establish Mardukite Babylonia and so forth—and then any of the higher applications of this, we'll be getting into in terms of Grade-III when we talk about "*The Tablets of Destiny*."

The same with, "How does Marduk assume the Fifty Names?" This is, of course, done by usurping the tradition *by agreements*—by Divine Right and going before the Assembly and saying: "If I can put the Cosmos in Order and into shape and make this a sustainable environment, you know, can I get the recognition for that?" That's part of the *Enuma Eliš* as well.

And then: "What is the function of the Maqlu Tablet series?" That's dealt with as the Tablet-M series of not only the [*Complete*] "*Anunnaki Bible*" or your "*Complete Anunnaki Legacy*" that is the Grade-II textbook, but also in the pocket hardcover edition, "*The Maqlu Ritual Book.*" This is an annual gathering—an annual... [*laughs*] I don't want to say "celebration." But an observance—a ceremonial observance—that was conducted by the priests and lasted multiple days, at least overnight.

And it was like what you would see with, like, "Burning Man" or the "Wicker Man" tradition in Druidism or what have you—it's a time when all of the illness, all of the malevolence, all of the dark spirits; everything is banished away, burned up—lots of different rituals are employed; creating various figurines and *doing things* to them. When you consider, for example, even the idea of the "voodoo doll" and things of that nature, you can find elements of that all the way back into the *Maqlu Tablets* and cuneiform texts.

Now, moving on through the "*Liber-L*" tablets and the "Question Review" that pertains to that, the first question: "What are the functions of the Priest-Kings, Scribe-Priests and temple servants?" Well, obviously, this is to maintain the Anunnaki traditions; but more to the point, to maintain the systematization of the society.

It always usually comes back to "control," but you have to understand there's a difference between "control" as it is able to assist people, assist their own survival and actually *help* an individual—such as you see with, for example, "Piloting" and "Piloted Processing" in upper-grades of Systemology; and the type of "enforced control" and just blatant misuse of the various ways in which in the individual *can* be programmed, imprinted upon and given reactive-response mechanisms.

I mean, the same "Tech" that can *undo* these things has been used for thousands of years to actually *do* them and install them—and this is why it was fairly easy, once we kinda caught into the groove of this, from Grade-II into Grade-III and upwards, in how this developed and how to resolve this.

Because, it's basically "reverse engineering" the Human Condition as it was installed by these Anunnaki figures that set up these "systems"—systems in consciousness, systems in Mind-programming, and the manner of language, the cuneiform script, the inclusion of language and the civic use *of* language to set up "codes" and so forth. None of which is inherently "bad," but again, we're talking about systems that are simply "operative systems"—they are not "good" or "bad" in themselves—they can easily be used or controlled or commanded by whoever has the authority and the knowledge to execute that.

"Describe the manner in which the favor of Marduk is won and lost in Babylon." We discussed that a little bit already in the Master Course, where those Kings that were observing the proper tradition—going all the way back to Alalu—those who are observing the traditions, those who are tending to the people, those who are actually assuming responsibility for positions that they're carrying, they do *fairly well*; and then those that simply get lost in the fragmentation of what some of those roles can contribute to, well, they *don't* do so well.

In the Babylonian Mardukite Tradition, the tablets refer—as far as the.. what's referred to on the King Lists, and then what we see with the actual prayers and hymns and different records left by the Kings themselves—those that felt the "Hand of Marduk" assist them *in* capturing Babylon or overtaking Babylon *from* those were *not* handling those positions of power so well, felt they had been in direct contact with Marduk; that they were given the graces and blessings and empowerment by Marduk to basically go a retake Babylon in his name.

Another point of discussion the significance about the zodiac cycles and ages having on the human experience: I mean, this operates on multiple levels. Obviously, those that occupied in the Age of Taurus—during the Sumerian age—experienced a totally different worldview than those operating, or existing, in the Age of Aries—during the time of the Mardukites and the Babylonians, and all of that was taking place during that time...

Different from those that have, for example, operated in the Age of Pisces, after, for example, the last two-thousand years, since the time of Jesus. These are points, right in themselves, you don't really need to dig into too far of what "astrological" symbolism is, to see that these "ages" have a particular *affect* on an individual. And of course, this has later been systematized into various forms of "astrology," but really it's an observation of cycles and patterns.

Next one: "Why might systematic fragmentation, or system fracture, been activated in Babylon?" Well, as we know, the position that Babylon had in the face of being right in the heart of "Enlilite" civilization or geography and terrain, this "control"—the proper execution of it happened for such a short period of time. These particular apex points, for example, of King Hammurabi, or Nebuchadnezzar II—these are points when Babylon reached the epitome of its glory. And you see that in these reconstruction efforts and during this renaissance periods; there's a lot of momentum and energy.

And then, for example, Hammurabi and Nebuchadnezzar—these are individuals that spent *forty-odd* years as Kings in these efforts, in these developments efforts and moving all this energy in this way. And then once they had done so and they had passed, those that ended up coming in thereafter very seldom were—they were pretty much spoiled. They were seldom able to execute the same fortitude, the same Self-Honesty, the same devotion and dedication that had been carried by those that had *actually* accomplished all these great feats along the way.

And so you see a lot of "back and forth"—and this doesn't even bring in the Anunnaki aspects, as far as the "Tower of Babel" and the *Erra Epos* and all the attacks on Babylon—everything to basically keep it from, really, during that entire Age of Aries, ever maintaining the type of, for example, reaching the epitome of a Grade-II work and bringing people to what we now treat as Grade-III.

So—that's why we treat the ancient Mardukite tradition as Grade-II; because, what they were reaching for, but what was never actually *realized* at that juncture, is what we now treat as Grade-III.

And then, one of the other points here, asking about the "birth of the Hermetic systems and the progression of occult magick" and how it aided in solidifying the systems: and we've almost described that here throughout the entire

Mardukite Master Course, concerning the epitome of what the Knowing and the launch and inception of the Ancient Mystery School; and then, for example, even what we've just discussed concerning fragmentation, but the de-evolution and fragmentation of the same, as it progressed through time and across vast distances of space and geography and multiple cultures all having a hand in it.

All of this, basically, leading to more and more solid fixed systems within the material understanding—either a Grade-I, or barely breaking into Grade-II, understanding, where, what I was talking about before, the "Great Mystery Box"—where all of these have kinda led to, rather than leading *out* of this system, they've just led one into circling around and around and around their own paradigms, and with no greater understanding achieved.

Then one of the questions from "*Liber-9*"—"How do Humans propagate the polar existence of evil and demons?"—and this is something we see reflected, again, in the applications and concepts of "demons" and "spirits" and how they apply to the Human Condition, the way it's set down in cuneiform writing. And, what most individuals have done—and most of this was meant to be allusions to a higher "Hermetic" philosophy, or what we get into in Systemology or Grade-III—but what most individuals have done, is treated this kind of information from a Grade-I perspective.

And so, they're treating these—you know, the concept of "demons" and all of this malevolence—as "entities," as "identities," and therefore giving *that* power. One of the ways in which this is reinforced within the tradition—and again, one of the *trappings* of it—is by putting too much emphasis *on* these other entities or individuals beings or "spirits" that affect the Human Condition.

Because, what we're referring to is not simply just "intelligent energies" out there—when we get into the idea of "demons" at *higher-level* Hermetic philosophy and spirituality and Systemology—because, it's not really dealt with directly *as* "demons"—but the concept behind it, is that an individual is basically fragmented, and whatever the personality-programming or whatever the implant is, or whatever the "command circuit" is, that is running—that is being put in stimulation—it's being treated as something separate from *Self*.

And so rather than taking command and control and responsibility and ability of it; it's an individual, kind of, stuck in a loop—so they have what we might consider "self-talk" with these kind of commands and directives and (quote; unquote) "voices" that are just simply this resonating speech or command pattern that's simply telling them something in one particular way or another; and it's an impinging thought—and this is actually just a high, heavy, solid level of fragmentation that an individual hasn't yet been able to face or *confront* directly.

And then, of course, the question: "How are the Lovecraftian elements and Cthulhu Mythos similar to Mesopotamia or different?"—I mean that in itself, I developed "*Liber-R*" and "*Liber-9*" as a way of, basically, rounding out the idea of what the "Necronomicon" and all these different presentations of it have represented.

But, the main point being: they're dealing with a planetary pantheon—so, you have all these correlations—and that's all in your materials there, as far as the way in which they correlate with one another. But, you have a planetary pantheon that's basically just given different names and the reason we don't deal with too much with it in the Mardukite Master Course is because it isn't specifically "Mesopotamian," which is our emphasis at Grade-II—but, it's the same principles.

And so once you already—I mean, we're already dealing with the Anunnaki pantheon, which is, in many ways, you know, different enough or outside the realm of the "norm" enough—even within the "New Age," which traditionally deal with other more familiar cultures.

So, we don't really try to focus too much on then, trying to make all the parallels to that. It's in the material—you can review that, as far as giving classes or discussion and so forth; it's just simply not something carrying forth. We're kind of emphasizing those points that have an application as we move up *higher* through the Grades in this course. The planetary assignment being one; the idea about the primordial development from the Nothingness—kind of a different version of a *Enuma Eliš*—but all given more of these darker "horror" overtones.

And then, of course, the concept of the "Gates"—the Gates that separate different existences, different forces and different levels of reality from other ones; and all being kept basically *from* this existence—but, it's kind of backwards, where: even though the Earth is pretty bad, or this physical universe is pretty bad, what the Lovecraftian paradigm is suggesting is that: what we're being *kept from* here, the forces and powers that are being *kept from* here—via these Gates and so forth—are basically what's allowing us to still continue to go on existing *here*; that for some reason, if these Gates were to be unlocked, if these forces were to be unleashed into this existence, that it would essentially bring the collapse of this existence.

There are many points here—where when we compare it to what we know of the various *Condensation of Universes* and even upper-level Systemology—we are seeing, again, an example of where these higher-level, higher, more actualized, beings—ones that are still in the position yet of *higher* points-of-view consideration from another dimension or Universe or existence, being able to impinge upon—and use the highest or strongest knowledge and technology and whatever demonstrations could be done in *this* universe, to basically come in and basically take over and take control and so forth.

And then, of course, the next logical step there, being the further *Condensation of Universes*, where once the former one has collapsed, and basically the enforcers come in to take over *this* one, then it just becomes a matter of time before *yet another* existence or Gate separates a further one, where we can separate and imprison those that don't seem to be agreeing with the order of *this* one.

: LECTURE 35—CORE REVIEW, PART II :
(September 28, 2020)

So Grade-II is a knowledge grade—it falls within the domain of, for example, the Mardukite Academy or within the domain of a "Wizard School." It is, essentially, a knowledge grade, a knowledge-level; we're dealing with "academic" studies still; we're dealing with "historical" references; we're dealing with an extension of "magic and mysticism."

The applications of it, beyond what was established as the Mardukite Chamberlains—which was the organization that contributed to the development of this Grade-II work and the Master Edition of "*Necronomicon: The Complete Anunnaki Legacy*"—the actual fundamentals can be applied in "Mardukite Zuism" *as* a spiritual or religious tradition in modern times that represents Mesopotamian Neopaganism.

That's why the completion—or, for example, at an academic level, or within the levels of your "Academy" or your instruction or working with Seekers—is still being treated as an intellectual pursuit; as a series of review and discussion questions, like we're going through, as a way of gauging knowledge and its achievement—the achievement of various ledges of knowing, which we'll deal with as we talk more about it in Grade-III.

This is to make certain that *they've*—that they've actually have achieved what is considered the Grade-II completion. And at this juncture, until we get to Grade-III and beyond, the way of grading this is really based on an intellectual level, as I'm explaining here. It's based on what an individual is able to perceive or *know*, given the last 6,000 years of knowledge, the last 6,000 years of technologies, the development of cultures, all of which we've covered up to this point, in the Mardukite Master Course.

Which, essentially, when we talk about "*The Great Magickal Arcanum,*" "*Merlyn's Complete Book of Druidism*" and "*Necronomicon: The Complete Anunnaki Legacy*"—those three volumes cover all the "Knowledge Grades" that basically introduce an individual, or get them up to the point, where what we are dealing with at Grade-III Systemology is completely accessible and in reach.

Otherwise, most individuals going straight for that, don't always find the same degree of effectiveness for it. To even put into the concept that—that, even when we're covering "*The Tablets of Destiny,*" that we're dealing with *cuneiform* tablets, that we're dealing with traditions that existed before, pretty much, all of what is explored, you know, in school or at a "Classical" level or in most movies and so forth.

And so, in order to have any kind of context or framework, we spend two complete grades, basically, flattening *6,000 years* of knowledge; both the knowledge of how it's been treated at the surface level of the world, and the knowledge as it existed in the underground, with various secret societies and classes of various priests and priestesses and lineages of Priest-Kings.

We've been able to trace this back—and so, in this lecture, what we want to do is continue the review of the "Mardukite Core" and basically just make sure we have a standardization of knowledge, before we start breaking into the upper-level applications of this—in terms of "Systemology."

One of the things we haven't really talked too much about within the Mardukite Master Course—most of which has been only today—has been the applications of, for example, the "Anunnaki Legacy" as it appears in the various factions of the "Magical Revival" and specifically, for example, the "Necronomicon."

This has been attached to "ceremonial magic" traditionally because of an individual named Kenneth Grant that kinda popularized the pursuit of it for his Ordo Templi Orientis—the OTO. And Kenneth Grant was one of the initiates or carriers of the "Crowley" tradition, and his development of it, however, was treated totally differently; he has a completely different take on methods of determining the powers in various names and numerological—gematria—and so forth.

What we end up finding is—really, it's not until more recently that we start to see these elements; because, for it to be connected directly to Aleister Crowley... At the time that he was really doing a lot of his explorations into "magical" work originally, and the developments he was most famous for, back at the beginning of the 20th Century, the concepts behind Babylonian and Sumerian tradition—such as we would explore them today at the level of Grade-II Mardukite work—was just not even, it wasn't even possible.

The material, the amount being translated or synthesized or even understood, outside of a few different scholarly realms—it just... That's what kind of puts our Mardukite work one step beyond that Grade-I pursuit; because, even though there may be allusions and there may be points-of-contact, different crossings or bridges that one could use—that we've even pointed out—within Grade-I work.

The Awareness and the knowledge just wasn't there. It may be that certain individuals, for example, Crowley *himself* may have pierced the veil into Grade-II—that's what's essentially... or the Second Gate—that's what's essentially being alluded to concerning his discovery of "*The Book of the Law*," but that doesn't mean that his knowledge and understanding was actually retained in its highest state, or even duplicated thereafter by those that read or practiced—other initiates and so forth.

The other reason being that—as far as connections to the

Sumerian and Babylonian tradition—Crowley's points of contact, and at the same time a lot of the imagery employed in Lovecraftian tradition and the origins of the Cthulhu Mythos and some of his other stories, kind of goes back to *Egypt* far more than it involves *Babylon*; mainly because—and we've discussed this—that the Egyptian (paradigm) was far more accessible, in terms of its lore, its artifacts, its position in Human Consciousness and how long it's been treated.

Whereas, a lot of the Assyrian tablets—the original cuneiform tablet discoveries—were only taking place during the middle and late 1800's. And then again, we had to deal with the material of time, various excavations being brought back to museums and universities, being transcribed, transliterated and then translated; and then even then being translated into native tongues first—the French and the Germans being the first two countries to excavate in Mesopotamia—and so a lot of the original texts transcribing the cuneiform tablets and the exploration of those that excavated them, were written in those languages.

And so, when someone does go to a university today and studies at that level—at a college level—anything that regards Mesopotamia or what they classify as Assyriology, French and German are two languages that are expected for an individual to take to complete that course.

What separated the "Simon Necronomicon"—the presentation of such at its time—from virtually everything else that was available on the occult scene, is that it wasn't derived from the Judeo-Christian—for example, the Kabbalah that has been established since then, which we discovered to be based on the Star-Gate system of Babylon—but it [*Simon's book*] wasn't based on that [*the Kabbalah*], such as you would find, for example, with the *Key of Solomon* or the *Goetia* or other traditional—even the *Book of Abramelin*—all of which is geared towards an understanding of mysticism or occultism, but from within the Judeo-Christian paradigm.

And so, it was really—it's still been those particular "grimoires," for example, the OTO, or the work of Aleister Crowley, or even the work of the "Golden Dawn" and similar practices; they've *all* operated within traditions that, basically, make their great explorations from the *Kabbalah* or the *Judeo-Christian* system—or basically the last 2,000 or 2,500 years of development along that stream specifically.

So, you see, for example, the "Tetragrammaton," the use of Hebrew and other elements of that appearing throughout "ceremonial magic" and the incantations; all of the grimoires. And so, what the "Necronomicon" represented, even for its—all of its—limitations back in the 1970's, was really an introductory view or peek into a paradigm that was *older* than that; that it was a different kind of "magic"—it alluded to a different kind of system that *predated* everything else that had been already explored or revived or treated, even at these "high-level"—supposedly "high level" ceremonial magic or "Hermetic Orders" and so forth.

In the works of Kenneth Grant, which are—it's referred to as the "Typhonian" trilogies, which is actually a series of nine books; three sets of three. The "Simon Necronomicon" is actually mentioned several times, and is referred to as the "*Schlangekraft* [*laughs*] *recension*," it's a German title, which is the name of the publishing company that originally released the "Simon Necronomicon" in its original hardcover form.

The original edition—the first edition—they were 666 copies, numbered copies, printed and bound; and those actually sold out based on magazine preorder [*ads*]. The idea that someone came out with this "Necronomicon"—it didn't take long for those to sell out.

And they (printed) a second edition—and actually, it's called the Silver Edition—and it's the more commonly seen one, when you're looking at the original hardcovers; we actually keep one in the vaults—and it was numbered of 3333, but it features a much more innate leather-bound cover, such as you might expect it to have more of that "eldritch" "cthonic" style.

But, particularly, in Kenneth Grant's book "*Outer Gateways,*" he makes mention of the "Simon Necronomicon" several times and also describes communications made by ceremonial magicians and magical lodges with these *Old Ones* or *Deep Ones* that he alludes to as having taken place; and this is something that we find in these "occult schools"—these "occult societies," academies, you know the "Hermetic Orders," and even the "Mardukite Tradition—all of them basically stemming from, at one point, this inner central core or an individual or a group or a "Higher Council" that is working with, or is in some kind of communication with some higher intelligence—or some inter-dimensional intelligence.

And this kind of contact with "alien entities"—so to speak—is very prevalent behind, the source behind, a lot of the resurgence of the "magical traditions" and the revivals of the last one-hundred and fifty years; it's just really not talked about.

So, there are many points where, for example, in Crowley or in examples of Kenneth Grant, that we see the Second Veil *pierced* many many times, but unfortunately because the presentation of it is always brought back to this Grade-I level of understanding, it seldom gets any individuals farther than that—and for that reason we were able to find the *limitations* to these mystical and occult gradients along the way—what eventually led us up to what we treat as Mardukite Systemology.

Keep in mind, during Lovecraft's literary career, he *never* actually published a book called the "Necronomicon"—nor was one ever delivered or presented to the public as such. It was basically this *archetypal* legendary book of epic proportions, really, that—it appeared as, almost as a character; it was almost its own character within the stories of H.P. Lovecraft—particularly those connected to the Cthulhu Mythos.

These stories—by the end of his life—these stories had, basically, made so many references to this book in so many different ways, that the idea that such a book could even exist—just based on its contents and its sheer size and everything almost seemed ridiculous. The irony of this being that your Grade-II "Mardukite Core" as its given in the Grade-II Master Edition, "*Necronomicon: The Complete Anunnaki Legacy*"—this is pretty much the only time that a book has ever been published with the title "Necronomicon" that lives up to the sheer, like I say, the mammoth [*laughs*] epic proportions of what it was to represent.

If the "Necronomicon" *was* to exist, the only one that has ever been presented, that could fulfill all of the criteria, would be the Grade-II textbook here: "*Necronomicon: The Complete Anunnaki Legacy.*"

One of the shortcomings of, for example, those that approached any time of resemblance of Grade-II type work outside of the Mardukite School—for example, in some of the others have kinda had brief glimpses and then taken it in their own directions. Anything connected to the "Necronomicon" will usually go back to, again, other than "Simon" version which is trying to redirect individuals to a Mesopotamian path—the Pathway of Mesopotamia—most of the other versions and any other references throughout history are always more geared back to a macabre, dark horrific, gothic nature of what Lovecraft describes.

To be honest with you, there's nothing to say that the universe—*this* dark universe and its outer reaches—is not in many elements the way that he describes. However, what ends up happening at a ritual level, or at a practical level, is that, for example, in—there's a magician that was very popular, a ritual magician in the 1990's named Donald Tyson that released a series of books called "Necronomicon."

These were meant to be practical magick occult ritual books —and the only reason they were effective is because they were actually based on the principles of "planetary magick" as they're set down in the "Hermetic" principles—the basic, even, classification that you would see with the Anunnaki, but rather than using the Anunnaki, it goes back, again, to using the pantheon—this Cthulhu Mythos—that Lovecraft developed and his perception of these *Elder Gods* and *reptilian beings* and monstrous creatures.

And of course, back of all this knowledge—I mean, all this still points in the direction, when we bring it to the individual, the Self—what we're doing in terms of Self-Actualization, returning command and control to the "I-AM" as the Alpha Spirit and so forth—we're talking about fragmentation of systems; we're talking about overcoming and getting through these systems and it's *that* realization that defines the Grade-II level or the Second Gate.

It's only once we've *actually* pierced into this next Gate that we have any understanding or conception of *what* the fragmentations actually are—what any of these systems *actually* are; that any of this is actually taking place. Because it's real easy to get all high and mighty and pompous and egotistical *at* a Grade-I level, and look down on to the Earth Gate and feel like you've got it all figured out—and *still* basically tied very heavily to the mechanisms *of* the Physical Universe, Beta-existence and Earth.

And so, at Grade-II, an individual is basically *piercing* the "veil" for the *first time*, no matter how many times they've supposedly traversed the "Spheres" or initiations or ceremonies to represent various "gate-openings" and so forth—it's only at a Grade-II level of realization that an individual *discovers* the nature of Self *having been* "entrapped" into a Human experience and all of the systems at play to provide that experience and so forth.

It doesn't mean that they have to completely understand it —this is something that is then, like I said, we deal with at Grade-III—which we'll be getting into here soon. But, what it does require is to know that it is there and it is *happening* —and that it is *possible* to *know* certain things, and that certain things exist.

By *that* realization and by rising above even that *lunar level* into the level of the "Hermetic" mysteries as they're treated as—not what you're familiar with in terms of "Hermetic Magic" and the schools of the Golden Dawn and all that; but the Hermetic mysteries as they were originally conceived of thousands and thousands of years ago *by* the priests of Nabu and the preservation and development of the Arcane Tablets as they're used throughout ancient Mesopotamia and its "magic" and its understanding of the Anunnaki and the Star-Gates and all of this.

This is the knowledge that brings us to a realization of *what* these Gates actually are, of what these beings actually are— what this fragmentation actually is—and then later, we can start dealing with the *actual* facing and handling and defragmenting of all these various facets; but it requires one just to have reached a level of understanding and knowledge and *knowing* of that *they* exist, that this is happening, that there *is* something to pursue—that there is something *beyond* just this lower-level treatment of knowledge in Grade-I or the ritualism and ceremonialism and even the National Religions and outer reflection of this, as it's presented in culture, for example, of Mesopotamia, because it's not the case that *every* individual occupying these various cultures or traditions that we've talked about over the last couple weeks, are actually achieving these higher levels of realization from that knowledge.

I mean, the same could be said, for example, where a lot of this was outlined when we had completed what was, at the time, the completion of the "Mardukite Core" in 2010—because really, it hasn't changed very much *after* that; it's just been the reorganization of *"The Anunnaki Bible."*

But, *"Liber-R"* was really meant to start *piercing the veil* on all this; to show higher level realizations that—or everything that I've described—and open up this idea about *Self, Self-Honesty*, the experience of *Self*, the programming aspects of that; and it's the first time we start treating it as the "programmed crystal" qualities or the "crystal fragmentation" or the ability of imprinting on different *facets* of a *crystal*, which you would then use as a "lens" to have an experience.

Later, we end up—ten years later—I revived this same idea when I released second main volume of Grade-III as *"Crystal Clear."* So, this concept—I mean, although it's taken a decade to reach a point of completion, for example, of the Mardukite Master Course and the three initial founding and "core" *Grades* of the Mardukite Academy and what this work that I've spent, now, twenty-five years—Earth years in *this* lifetime—developing as a literary record and as a tradition or a pathway.

The elements of it were, pretty much, laid out a decade ago in various texts and it's, you know, again: unless an individual—these have been available and very popularly and widely distributed in the underground—unless an individual is prepared to actually *face* this information and see this knowledge at a *higher* level than what they are traditionally used to, and all the background Grade-I experience they have—and all the "Magical Schools" and so forth—that these higher levels of realization wouldn't be accessed.

And this was expressed nearly a decade ago—*"Necronomicon Revelations"* and all that material in *"Liber-R"*—which you can go through more in depth, is all contained within the "Mardukite Core"—*"Necronomicon: The Complete Anunnaki Legacy"* as your Grade-II textbook.

The same as—I haven't gone into it nearly as much, in terms of this course, because we've already touched on it here and throughout—in terms of just delivering any kind of sense what this has been understood as in modern "magical revivals," but the "Simon Necronomicon." My explorations of that *after* writing "*Liber-R*" and, basically, capping off the "Mardukite Core" at that juncture.

I had *still* been getting so many letters—most of my *emails* at the time at the Offices—were still concerning, and these were people that had read "*Liber-R*," was still concerning the "Simon Necronomicon." I was presenting, you know, all of this work of the Mardukite Chamberlains, we had our "*Anunnaki Bible*"—I had already given my commentary in "*Necronomicon Revelations*" concerning the "Simon Necronomicon, as it applied and its background applications, the Kenneth Grant stuff—everything we've kind of discussed today—and again, I was *still* getting all these questions about "*How to make the Simon Necronomicon work.*"

I mean, most of my time a decade ago was completely engrossed *in* the "Necronomicon"—and *not* always *my own*. And so, what this ended up leading to is—I finally had to break silence again, and I released "*Liber-555*" and the interesting thing about that, which it really hasn't been expressed: just as "Liber-R" was really an extension of "*Liber-9*," the original title—instead of "Necronomicon Shadows" or "Nine Gates of the Kingdom of Shadows"—the original title the work that was gonna take place as an extension of "*Liber-9*" was going to be called "*Crossing to the Abyss.*"

And then—so, it was actually listed as a book that was going to be forthcoming at the time—and then, what we ended up doing is we said, "Oh, well, we're putting that on the backburner," and we ended up working on "*Liber-50*" and *that* one was not presented as, but it was announced the whole time that we were working on this project called "*Crossing to the Abyss.*" But then when "Liber-50" came out, it *wasn't* "Crossing to the Abyss."

So, finally, it was kind of a joke—as far as from the Offices—

but, the fact that I was returning again to the subject *of* the "Simon Necronomicon" and having to deal with that—and then the fact that we were moving beyond, again, I had already established in "*Liber-R*" where the Simon book and former understandings of it were leading. Finally, we just called "*Liber-555*," *Crossing to the Abyss* [laughs] and that is the Mardukite "guide"—it's an extension, again, of "*Liber-R*"—but it's the Mardukite "guide" to the "Simon Necronomicon."

And it's not meant to be a "companion" or "copy-cat" book of that nature, but it's literally after presenting all of this—the Mardukite "Necronomicon" and all of this work for the "Anunnaki Bible" and the "Mardukite Core," it still seemed that there was some unfinished business there. So, "*Crossing to the Abyss*"—which is also included in your Grade-II textbook—is really just a step-by-step commentary, from the Mardukite paradigm and from the paradigm or worldview, from the "Route of Mesopotamia" in Grade-II—examining the "Simon Necronomicon" point for point.

It doesn't replace the need to *have* a copy; we've never tried to *compete* in any way or overshadow that, but it's—again, too much time was spent in trying to answer these questions that a publication just had to be brought out to bring it all together and just to kinda put a final word out on that. And that was released, finally, in 2012 and is actually one of the more recent editions to the "*Mardukite Core*," when you really look at it.

Very little—I've said very little in the eight years, nine years, since—I've said very little, actually, about this subject, aside from various radio interviews and other workshop lectures and stuff; because, like I say, it is pretty much the final word regarding that.

And in terms of "*Necronomicon: The Complete Anunnaki Legacy*" and my career with the "Necronomicon"—publishing with the "Necronomicon"—it's pretty much been standardized with *this new* 2020 Master Edition and everything that's going to entail. From that, everything that we've been doing —or focused on—regarding Mesopotamia and Mesopotamian Neopaganism, is really geared more towards "Mardukite Zuism" and the "Founding Church of Mardukite Zuism," Mardukite Ministers within that tradition and the counseling services and spiritual advisement of its Systemology— that's where we're actually headed to, regarding any further developments.

Although the Mardukite Chamberlains—it still exists—really it's evolved into "Mardukite Zuism" and then as an intellectual pursuit, the "Mardukite Academy." Really, the Mardukite Chamberlains existed *while* we were developing—and as a research organization—*toward* the development of this Grade-II "Core."

Beyond that, we have—you know, we've outgrown the need for an exclusive exploration to put together this "Research Library." So, those individuals have actually moved toward "Mardukite Zuism" and "Systemology."

And all of the development at this point regarding ancient Mesopotamia, Mesopotamian traditions, the Anunnaki and using that towards Mesopotamian Neopaganism is going to fall under "Mardukite Zuism." And its the advanced work that we're now doing, in regards to "Systemology" and the work that we'll be getting into here in the next lectures and the next couple of days—to round out the Mardukite Master Course—all falls within the domain of "Mardukite Systemology."

And so, the "Systemology Society" is primarily made up of members of the Mardukite Alumni that had worked with us during the last decade in the development and pursuit of establishing the "Mardukite Core." Without establishing that "Core" and its evolution into, you know, shooting past that in its evolution into "Mardukite Systemology," we would not have this Master-level understanding that we do, or even be able to deliver a "Mardukite Master Course" for *these* three Grades.

And then, although it's not specifically a part *of* the Mardukite Master Course—it's not part of the "Mardukite Core" specifically, and it's not integrated in the Grade-I materials as far as the textbooks are concerned—there is, as an alternative, five years ago, prior to the [*public*] establishment of the Systemology Society, a group of the Mardukite Alumni; and this was a time when we were seeing a large revival interest in darksider traditions, cyber traditions, various elements of "Vampire" culture and the "undead"—all of this making a come-back in pop-culture, and along with that the occult mysticism and traditions that were attached to that.

So, I got together—and this was an underground project at first, and it's just slowly evolved into becoming "Moroii ad Vitam Paramus," which means "Living Vampires Preparing For a Second Life."

Now, the emphasis behind this was really toward the establishment of a Mesopotamian (slash) Egyptian "Book of the Dead" darksider tradition, drawing from the Cain and Lilith lore from Mesopotamia and kind of Vampyre tradition as it was carried other forms of "dark culture" and "dark tradition"; the elements of the "Kabbalah" and the Judeo-Christian tradition, how it evolved throughout the Middle Ages to the way the Church viewed "magic."

I mean there was a time when the word for "werewolf," "vampire" or "witch" all meant basically the same thing in Europe. And so, there's a lot of crossings between these various—the concepts behind these various traditions—and this is something that, really, although I had my *own* involvement with it and different cultures and different things that were going on back in the 1990's—you know, just a different time—it wasn't something that I had to dealt with very much in my own writings; and something that I had kind of steered away from many many times.

But again, just like returning to the subject of the "Simon Necronomicon," there was a point where enough of this had been brought to my attention that I said, "Well, let's really take a look at this." So a bunch of Alumni got together and started working on this as a precursor of what has eventually evolved into Grade-III "Mardukite Systemology."

In the "Vampyre Tradition," we're dealing with—well, one of the ways in which it can be treated for *fun*, it could be treated as a *tradition*, it could be treated as an alternate form of *culture*—but, the trappings therein, again, being the elements of the Physical Universe; any kind of "magic" or "mysticism" or "energy work" that is still keeping one tied to the *body*; anything that's not removing emotional imprinting—a lot of this is very high level work, because if you aren't already a bit actualized, you're basically compounding and supercharging the tendencies and emotional reactivity and programming that you already have.

So, you're dealing with energy flows, you're dealing with the "rays"—you're dealing with the "Dark Side" underbelly of culture, the way it's being treated from the surface world—you know, all these "dark beings" and "creepy crawlies" of the night and so forth, undead traditions.

And then back behind that, again, we're talking about the "Other." We're talking about "death" and "transition" points as going *beyond* these elements—and of course, the concepts of "Immortality" and the *Ankh* and the connection between Heaven and Earth—or the Spiritual and the Physical and all the representations.

You'll deal a lot with the Egyptian Tradition and its concepts of "death" and the "afterlife," the "Book of the Dead" or the "Coming Forth and Rising" into these higher planes of existence, the way that it's treated as basically an extension of the "Ladder of Lights" of Mesopotamia.

So, it isn't *actually* absolutely critical for bridging between

Grades—between Grade-II and Grade-III—or for working with "Mardukite Systemology." It's just something that *is* available; and the two works that were developed for that—the "*Vampyre's Bible*" and the "*Cybernomicon*"—now both appear in "*The Vampyre's Handbook,*" this Fifth Edition hardcover collector's edition that we released this year from The Joshua Free Imprint.

And so, there's all the materials that were—it was considered "*Liber-V*" when it came out as "*Book of V*" and what I ended up treating in, or rather what wasn't treated in "*The Vampyre's Bible*" ended up being held for another book, the "*Cybernomicon.*" It was originally intended to be *one* specific volume and since we had already referred to the first book "*Vampyre's Bible,*" it was hard to call the anthology of the two of them "*Vampyre's Bible.*"

So, the "*Vampyre's Handbook*" kind of goes along with the tradition of these hardcover practical guide handbooks, where we have: "*The Vampyre's Handbook,*" we have "*The Sorcerer's Handbook,*" we have "*The Druid's Handbook.*" I have a couple other "handbooks" actually planned for the future

And then, it just so happens to be that the huge Grade-III Master Edition textbook for Systemology is called "*The Systemology Handbook*"—although it's definitely not a small portable handbook, it's the complete anthology of all materials for Grade-III in one book.

So, that *in* a nutshell *is* Mardukite Mesopotamian tradition and everything that we've presented for that; and everything beyond that is a bridge and entry-point into Grade-III "Mardukite Systemology."

: LECTURE 36—THE TABLETS OF DESTINY :
(September 28, 2020)

The Mardukite Master Course is so defined because of a "Master" level of understanding that is applied to what we consider the Master Grades—*Grade-I*, *Grade-II* and *Grade-III*. And so, the Master Course—in Grade-I, we had two textbooks that, basically were meant to establish, and *flatten*, all of the mystery surrounding "magick and mysticism" and "Druidism" and all of the "enchantments" and the "Faerie World" and the "Dragon Legacy" and all of that; and they kind of go together to solidify the *foundation* of what Grade-I material and Grade-I understanding *is*.

And in Grade-II, we are treating, of course, the "Mesopotamian Paradigm"; we're treating the application of cuneiform tablets and the pantheon of the Anunnaki as was understood within the Mardukite Babylonian Tradition—and it is from this that we ended up discovering many of the elements of what we were after to achieve a *higher* point of realization and break forth into that *Third Veil*—that *Third Gateway*—of *Understanding* and *Knowing*.

That it was actually already *right there* within the "Arcane Tablets," so long as an individual was, basically, empowered —or given the ability, or the illumination—to identify these points and to actually see where this was going; to be able to go back and not just do a "reconstruction" of, you know, the "Ancient Mesopotamian" or "Mardukite" tradition as it was observed in ancient Babylon—and not simply do some revival of some 4,000 or plus year tradition; but to take an actual Self-Honest look at what they were doing and what has unfolded since then, and the "Big Picture" of Grade-I and Grade-II and perhaps even where they had come from—but that information had been lost along the way and then reduced to this, kind of, symbolic religio-spiritual mystical methodology.

So, just as the textbooks—"*The Great Magickal Arcanum*" and "*Merlyn's Complete Book of Druidism*"—really go together to form that complete foundation, the establishment of all of our future work: the work beyond Grade-III—the work from the Mardukite Academy and the Systemology Society and beyond—is really built upon the next two tiers on this *Pathway* and that's a combination of Grade-II and Grade-III work; because the overlapping understanding there being, again, ancient Mesopotamia and these Arcane Tablets.

And so, although it wasn't released as such—within the Mardukite Core period—luckily in developing the full Mardukite Master Course, "*Mardukite Zuism: A Brief Introduction*"—this was a booklet that Kyra Kaos and I had established when we were going to structure and formulate the "Mardukite Zuism" path as an extension of where things had come with our Mardukite work as the Chamberlains, and at the same time establishing Systemology.

That is—we discussed that information and *that* is actually a part of "*Necronomicon: The Complete Anunnaki Legacy*"—that is a part of its introduction; we discussed that *last week* in one of those lectures. And in essence, although it was essentially the *last thing* to be included for Grade-III—it's actually *also* included in the Master Edition of the Grade-III textbook, which is "*Systemology Handbook*," and that includes all of the material up until the most recent work—I mean, we're talking within the last few months "work"—all of that material that was developed in the last decade for the field of Systemology.

Now, in addition to "*Mardukite Zuism: A Brief Introduction*," which is how "*The Systemology Handbook*" is actually introduced, because it was established along with, again, "Mardukite Zuism"—the work concerning Systemology as it applies to Mardukite Zuism, when we're talking about the advanced counseling, "processes" and "ministerial work," is basically geared towards two publications: "*The Tablets of Destiny*" and "*Crystal Clear*"—those are the two publications from *The Joshua Free Imprint* that appear as stand-alone (titles), but of which also (are) compiled in "*The Systemology Handbook.*"

And this "*Systemology Handbook*" Master Edition—again, this is another "beefy" textbook that includes *literally* all of the work and all of the development and background work going back almost a decade now *of* the modern Systemology Society.

So, for the purposes of our Mardukite Master Course, we're of course going to go through everything that entails, because this is the Master Edition—but, in regards to Mardukite Zuism, the main elements are "*The Tablets of Destiny*" and "*Crystal Clear.*" And other than "*Mardukite Zuism: A Brief Introduction,*" as a booklet, you know, so it could be easily distributed, the point of transition between (Grade-II) and Grade-III is "*The Tablets of Destiny*" (the publication).

This is, essentially, an access point that anyone that's been working through this can use, but if you even want to give it to your Seekers as even a Grade-II "graduation-completion" *gift* or something of that nature—"*The Tablets of Destiny,*" although it is not the *first* publication or the *first* work on "Systemology" ever developed, all of the other (previous) work was first developed underground.

A little over—about a year ago, I guess it is—"*The Tablets of Destiny*" was released and its designation is "*Liber-One.*" And the idea there being, originally, all of the specific "Mardukite Chamberlain Grade-II Type" Mesopotamian materials for the Mardukite Core—or, you know, the [*Complete*] "*Anunnaki Bible*"—were intended as having "letter designations," such as "*Liber-N*" for the "*Necronomicon*" or "*Necronomicon Liturgy and Lore*" we had "*Liber-L.*" Kind of like what I was mentioning before, with "*Liber-9*"—because, "*Liber-9*" was meant to include more than the three or four "Tablet" series that was included in the [*Complete*] "*Anunnaki Bible*"—it was actually intended to include the material from "*Necronomicon Revelations*," what was eventually released later as "*Liber-R*."

But the original designation of "*Liber-9*" [with the intention that it would have included "*Liber-R*"]—the original idea was that the "Systemology" publications, and in that case, a "crossover" or "gateway to the other side"; or "crossover" being "*Liber-9*"—that *all* of our "Systemology" publications would have "numeric" designations to, kind of, differentiate them.

For example, with "*Arcanum*" we have "*Liber-A*." And even the "Vampire" work—"*The Vampyre's Handbook*" as "*Liber-V*." Any of the work that was specifically going to be Systemology—which "*Necronomicon Revelations*" is: part describing "esoteric grimoires" and part describing *our* "Systemology"—they were going to have numeric designations.

So, "*Liber-One*" is "*The Tablets of Destiny*" and "*Crystal Clear*" (we discussed briefly the existence of that there) it's "*Liber-2B*"—as in "*to be or not to be*." So, "*Liber-2B*" is "*Crystal Clear*" and the text for both of those appear in your Grade-III textbook, there, the Master Edition hardcover 2020 "*Systemology Handbook*."

I want to talk about then—we're going to get into Grade-III or transition to Grade-III using "*The Tablets of Destiny*" text; because, if you've been following along—and *most of the individuals here*, I mean this has become... you've probably read this book several times now—but...

An individual following along, or a Seeker being brought through the Mardukite Master Course sequence of material—the way that I've delivered it—the type of material that we're dealing with in Systemology, which is actually quite advanced and far reaching, in comparison, for example, to the first steps of "ritual magic" and so forth; if you've been following along the progressive *Path* that I've laid out here, the gradients are such a *smooth progression* that *this is* the next logical step, and what's presented here is not going to seem like a "foreign language." It begins right *in* the heart of Mesopotamia.

Now, in regards to archaeology and in regards to historical documents or historical artifacts or museum-quality type of material that scholars and academicians are going to explore, "The Tablets of Destiny" are for all intents and purposes, in regards to Anunnaki mythology, it's really—I mean, we might as well just call this the "Necronomicon." But, without employing "Lovecraftian" overtones.

"The Tablets of Destiny" are this, you know, hugely *enigmatic* powerful facet of the ancient Sumerian tradition and they appear in Babylonian literature. These have *yet* to be actually brought forth, so what we have done—as far as the Systemology Society—is go in an uncover what the *actual*... well, there is: the "*systemology*" of what this actually represents; and that became the basis of what is now the Grade-III (Mardukite) Systemology work.

This concept of the "Tablets of Destiny," if you remember, is introduced in the *Enuma Eliš*—in the "Epic of Creation" and complete backbone of Mardukite Babylonia; and it's these Tablets of Destiny that essentially represent the *Power*, the *Order*, the *Law*—of Tiamat, which she then distributes to Kingu, which Marduk is then able to take, and then using that, becomes the "New Order"—the new "figure" that is, basically, putting the "Cosmos" into *shape*; dividing the "Spiritual" from the "Physical" and the fragmentation of the "Universe" and all that.

It's demonstrating—the story—this isn't to say that Marduk is necessarily the "one" responsible for all of that, but in the Mardukite Tradition, Marduk *is* the "One" who *knows* this knowledge, who *knows* the Way—and basically "beheld" the "Tablets of Destiny" and put things into the Order that they are, and thus understands—understands how *we* got *here*; understands how *we* get *back*.

The "Tablets of Destiny" are meant to distinguish a "Cosmic Law" or "Divine Law" that *orders* the *systems* of, for example, what we consider "Universes." Whereas another type of "Tablet of Destiny" or "Tablets of Fate" in cuneiform literature, and they represent something more akin to what we might consider the "Book of Life"—where an individual's name is inscribed in there, and all of their deeds are recorded and so forth; which is actually what we're dealing with when we're dealing with "imprinting" and "fragmentation" and so forth; what's being carried along with us and which actually shapes our "personality" and shapes our "actions," and beliefs and knowledge; which of course, further shapes our considerations until we've, of course, come down to this Human Condition as we have it.

And then this of course brings up the idea, for example, as "records"—being the idea that a "Book of Life" are *records* of all that was and is and such; the formation of systems, this calls into mind, for example, from other Grades or other traditions, the idea of "Akashic Records"—this "timeline" or "time-track" of which all of existence is, kind of, *moved* through and along with it, the considerations of—well, for example, *of Self*, as it's experienced each of these *variations*.

And, of course, we know that these "Levels" and "Veils" are *alluded* to in other esoteric symbolism—such as the "Kabbalah" and the "Gates" and so forth—and that they represent, essentially, the "divisions" of what is composing the Human Condition.

So, by the time we get into "Systemology," we're dealing a lot with *semantics*, vocabulary—the actual meaning behind things—because it becomes *that much* more critical. That's another one of the "keys" that you can actually take out of Grade-II, when it comes to cuneiform literature; the actual systematization of knowledge and knowing and experience and thinking, in terms of "words" and "vocabulary" and that "shift" in consciousness. That's one of the revelations out of Grade-II material.

And so, in the "Introduction" to, for example, "*The Tablets of Destiny*" or as it appears in the complete Grade-III textbook —"*The Systemology Handbook*"—we discuss the actual cuneiform tablets, we discuss the "Tablets of Destiny" and history very briefly in the "Introduction" to *introduce* the framework of what we're going to be handling.

For example, the word for "*fate*" is NAM; and then for "*destiny*" is NAM-TAR, and that means to "*cut fate*" or to *cut* NAM—so NAM-TAR—or to "ordain" or "decree." And so, when you think about this, it's very interesting—and I've pointed this out long before we even established a text called "*The Tablets of Destiny*," though I forget exactly where.

But, it is very interesting to me, when it comes to "*destiny*" and "*fate*"—these two concepts—that the cuneiform language, as it was written, would actually *differentiate* these two. I mean, we're talking about a language where the word for "eye"— for example, with the IGIGI "*Watchers*"—the word for "*eye*," the word for "*see*" and the word for "*watch*" and all that, was all the same word; whereas obviously there is meant to be a distinction between the words "*fate*" and "*destiny*" and such, as what we consider a "primitive language," would even distinguish the word-signs of these two concepts.

The way I've been explaining it—since the very first "Mardukite Systemology" courses, going back to, I believe, either late 2008 or early 2009, when I was setting down the "*Reality Engineering*" lectures for the first time—*Destiny*, just by, you know, we deal a lot with semantics and word origins in our intellectual study (keep in mind that we're maintaining a literary tradition almost in honor of the scribe-priests of Borsippa within the domain of Babylon)—when we're dealing with the idea of *Destiny*, it should be almost apparent, given the root word there, that we're talking about a "*destination.*"

We're talking about the point *to* which a particular course is being traveled; and the *Destination* is a "fixed" point. Now, the way that you might *go to arrive* at that, that's another story, that might be multiple (possible) routes, and that is what we generally refer to as "*fate*," which has more to do with the *nature* of the *Pathway* on which you're traveling or, for example, the Game—the Game of Life.

Fate is *ruled* by *Destiny*, because "*Destiny*" is the firm, standard, fixed—the "ends" so to speak, or the "definitions" of the Game; whereas an individual's "*Fate*" is mainly determined by their own inclinations, their own choices and decisions *within* the confines of the *greater* Game.

It's really this point, when we're talking about "Destiny" and we're talking about the "Tablets of Destiny," we're talking about the *End Goals*; we're talking about the *Pathway* that leads to *Infinity*; we're talking, essentially, that which is *what* the *Ordering* of the *Cosmos* is structured around and those systems.

We're not dealing necessarily in "absolutes"; but we're dealing closely in *that* direction; whereas "*fate*" is really a matter of an individual's experience—it's really, when it comes to the Human Condition, of course that experience, the freedom of choice, is really based on an individual's ability to be *free* of all the imprinting and response-mechanisms that are fixed upon them [or that *they* are fixed upon].

But, this difference between *Destiny* and *Fate* is how "*The Tablets of Destiny*" material is introduced. It's basically introduced with a language lesson by one of our Staff Writers that deals with the Mesopotamian aspects of Systemology—Reed Penn.

It's important for me to illustrate that as we get into this, because there is a distinct *connection* between the cuneiform language and Mesopotamia *and our* presentation of the "Tablets of Destiny" as being a launch point from out of this, you know, "archaic tradition" that has already been so obscure that we dedicate an entire textbook—an entire grade—to the "Route of Mesopotamia" and then *from this* we are pulling out elements to illustrate a higher level of understanding of which you can then, of course, go back and review and find elements of all this.

But, we're talking about *here*, just a very basic—the significance behind this, more than just trying to define terms for an individual about, "Oh what is *destiny?* What is *fate?*"— we've reached a point where there really are no arbitraries in this respect. I'm communicating to you in a spoken language that is represented in a particular culture, which is English, and it's written down—or it's gonna be transcribed in a specific way, which is English.

These particular words are meant to duplicate an understanding that I am trying to communicate *by* delivering these messages; and the meanings behind them, once it gets into the "other end"—once it's reached the receiver—we're dealing with, essentially, a whole different reality; we're dealing with an individual's... we're dealing with *you* and *you...* and *you... all your* "personal universes" as this is being received—and whether or not it's actually one-to-one with what I'm projecting is another story. [*Laughs*]

But, *this* is the first lesson in that—in the very "Introduction" of "*The Tablets of Destiny*" we're differentiating a distinction between *Destiny* and *Fate*; and an individual that, for example, with this basic, you know, semantic lesson is already stumbling over that—this type of... the ability to differentiate, the ability to understand the meanings intended behind one word or another—this is very critical for a Master-Level understanding of Systemology.

Even at a Grade-III level—we're not even, at this point,

gonna be dealing with any *upper-level* Grades, or the... anything specific for "Mardukite Ministers" that is not already reflected in *this* textbook—anything regarding "Piloting"—I just plan on taking the rest of the Mardukite Master Course to deliver the Grade-III Mardukite Systemology *as it's* presented in the books—in the textbooks—and how you might treat it in "courses" in your Academies, or when working with your Seekers, regarding the application of this material at a personal level, while still regarding it at an "academic-school" level.

The point when we break here (is) between the Systemology presented in the Mardukite Master Course and the Systemology that we deal with at higher levels or other forms of training—such as the Flight School, which is geared towards Piloting. And "Piloting" is a specific application of the principles that we're going to be spending *the next couple days* covering.

I'm not holding anything back from what's relayed in the material—but, before an individual attempts to *apply* this to "Piloting" and actual "processing" and "spiritual advisement" aside from simply having a Master-Level understanding of this material as an instruction, as a background to "Mardukite Systemology." We want to focus them on *this* mastery first, before trying to take this to that practical level.

And an individual should be able to work *through* this textbook—"*The Systemology Handbook*"—and be able to understand it and apply it to themselves and be able to instruct others in the material specifically that this covers, within the domain of the Mardukite Master Course and the first three "Grades" of the Mardukite Academy of Systemology.

"Piloting" however, is a completely separate aspect—as is what we'll be treating as "Mardukite Zuism" and the "ministry" and "religious" aspects of that as a completely separate aspect of this—(we're focusing) simply (on) the treatment *of this* Grade-III "Mardukite Systemology" material as *information*; as *knowledge*.

A lot of time is spent in *"Tablets of Destiny"*—in that textbook, and of course, within the entire Master Edition of it as well, *"The Systemology Handbook"*—but, as *"Liber-One"* and as the main bridge between what we we're treating as the "Route of Mesopotamia" and the Mardukite Chamberlains and the development of the Mardukite Organization over a decade *and* the Grade-III work of Mardukite Systemology and the Systemology Society and the evolution of Mardukite Zuism, we're treating *semantics* a lot—we're treating the definitions, defining the concepts, making sure that before we start piercing these *higher* levels of understanding, even within the Grade-III work, that we are making sure an individual doesn't go past a point that they don't understand.

This a key point of delivering the Mardukite Master Course at *any* Grade, when you're handling Seekers or when you're representing it—to make sure that an individual isn't moving past a point they don't understand; because, although it may continue to be quite interesting—although they may continue to read or continue to attempt to apply the attention, as much as they can will—the actual *Awareness* begins to dim, because they've already missed something and they're just moving past and going through the motions of reading words, but not actually comprehending and not actually carrying within them what they had achieved up until that point. Honestly, it just kinda gets left off right there, and until an individual goes back and picks it up and goes through whatever it is that they misunderstood, there's no further realizations that are going to be achieved from that, in which to base another level or gradient of understanding.

So keep in mind, I mean, really at the first levels, you know, the primary elements of Systemology—especially at a Grade-III level within the Mardukite Master Course—we're still in the domain of Mesopotamia, but we're treating it a little bit differently; and as we go along, we're *defining* things… Including, for example, when we talk about the Mardukite Paradigm: the idea that a *paradigm* is simply an "all-encompassing standard in which to view the world; a worldview" and then also to communicate reality—it's something you use to represent objects, it's something used to associate other knowledge with; and then others that are in a shared reality, to be able to communicate that same thing. That's what a *paradigm* is.

So, when we're talking about the "Mardukite Paradigm," we're talking about the idea of going back 4,000 years from the Mesopotamian worldview—the view in which to experience the world—and looking at the *Enuma Eliš*, the Epic of Creation, the idea of the "Ordering of the Cosmos"; all of that takes place from the "Infinity of Nothingness" and everything that we've covered in Grade-II, but now in this *new* elevation of the same Mardukite Core, we're going back and actually making certain that we can establish a higher level of understanding from this.

And so, this even goes into making certain that we're *defining* things—and especially those that are being introduced to this for the first time. Because it's not automatically expected that all individuals coming into the Academy or taking courses—I mean, unless you have prerequisites for this—or those that discover the books, since they are available… I mean, you can get these wherever books are sold—that an individual is going to have the background that we've established through the *last week and a half* of the Mardukite Master Course.

It's really up to your abilities as Master-Level Instructors to be able to gauge that and work that out with your own applications; because, you know, if we were just to make it where every individual *had to* go through "ritual magic school" in order to become a "Mardukite Zuist" or *every* individual had to go through the studies of "Mesopotamia" and choose "Mardukite Zuism" in order to get benefit from "systemological processing," well, I mean, that would be ridiculous.

Now, it's a little bit different here [*laughs*] when we're talking about the Mardukite Master Course, because this particular course—the appendices of these Master Editions; the fact that we've collected all this stuff together as "Master-Level Grades" and are delivering an "Instructor's Manual" to you and eventually transcripts of this overview of understanding that hasn't necessarily been laid directly *in* the former texts—that's a little bit different.

We're treating *this* Master Course as, basically, an Instructor's Level of education to be able to go and administer "education" and "assistance" in these types of traditions and this kind of work and with Seekers and even establish branches of the Mardukite Academy or the Systemology Society on your own—and be able to actually do that effectively and with access to the same work, you know, these same editions that we use at the Library at the Academy; with access to, for example, these lectures, the information that I can best easily give directly, knowing that an individual already has access to these other materials and is already working at it as an encompassing whole, as opposed to the individual parts or routes.

This is what is making the Mardukite Master Course essentially the upper-most epitome of what we've been able to develop—of what *I've* been able to develop, actually—in twenty-five years of working at this special education for Instructors or a Master-Level education for Seekers that, you know, wished to work through all this on their own—which is also perfectly fine, as long as you have the dedication and fortitude to push through all of these points and get through the bulk of material unaided by any direct assistance. Even the formation of "study groups"—where everyone is working individually, but then also together from the same bodies of material and the same outlines—can be incredibly beneficial in working through this material.

We mentioned a bit about, for example, the Necronomicon; we mentioned a bit about the way that Babylonian magic even developed into the "Kabbalah"; and the "Kabbalah" (even) developed into other traditions of "magic" and "grimoires" and so forth—so, even within, when we're dealing with the cuneiform tablets or the "Arcane Tablets" as the apply to Systemology, we're always dealing with the same "objective reality"—we're dealing with the same *things* "out there," we're dealing with the same "tablets."

We're dealing with the same pieces of material—the difference being our *"level of understanding."* And we kinda throw this around a lot—I mention it a lot fluidly in the vocabulary of the Mardukite Master Course—and usually this is related in connection to the "Gates" and to the *Three Grades* of the Mardukite Master Course as we've relayed it.

So, for example, at our *first level of understanding*, whether we're dealing with cuneiform tablets—such as the *Enuma Eliš*—or we're dealing with any other kind of practices or traditions, we're mainly dealing with "surface magic"; we're dealing with that Grade-I level of understanding that—even if it isn't Grade-I; it could even be Grade-O [*zero*] for that matter—it could be just *whatever* the "exoteric," you know, the "common denominator"—just the base level understanding that the average member of the population would carry.

And, I mean, this can include all manner of using "prayers" and "devotion" and treating the Anunnaki as "deities" and "idols" and so forth; and it also tends to lead to a lot of "cultural superstition" [*also indicative of the early lunar-cults of Sumer*], which tends to, kind of, overshadow any of the truer elements that may be actually hidden within a particular application of cultural mythology or some kind of practices.

So, that's the *"exoteric"* understanding. And then the *"esoteric"* understanding—when we approach the *second level of understanding*—we're talking about, for example, Grade-II; we're talking about the *systematization* of an *understanding*, for example, as represented by the god Nabu, the Anunnaki deity that's considered the Speaker or the Prophet; the one that's the heir or herald of the Mardukite Tradition and establishing a standard in Babylon in honor *of* his father Marduk.

And this is all done, of course, as the son of the essential hero *of* the *Enuma Eliš* and the representation thereof—this idea of representing in the priesthood and whatnot; but we're talking about the *esoteric* way in which those that were the learned—for example, with the written word and the Hermetic philosophies, and for example, the way in which we've treated the information of ancient Mesopotamia *directly as* "The Route of Mesopotamia."

Once we've, kind of, gotten an individual through the whole "Mystery" of the "magic" and "enchantments" at the Grade-I (level), we don't necessarily have to treat Mesopotamia at that level; and so, in the Grade-II work and the Mardukite Core, we were really treating it as a literary tradition and an intellectual tradition in a way in which individuals were able to elevate their Awareness and their experience and their view of the world—and their relationship with that—by simply having a *higher* understanding at an intellectual level, in terms of language, being able to set down the vocabulary, the semantics.

And so, what this inevitably leads to is, now that we've gone through all that—and all the material from, for example, "*Necronomicon: The Complete Anunnaki Legacy*"—we've, more or less, established and *flattened* the nature and function *of* that "Mystery School" as well.

What we're left with is, basically, anything that we can take from it that's not specific to any of the cultural paradigms—or any specific religious dedication and so forth—but to look at, beyond that, what the Priests were actually knowing and what the Priesthoods were actually after, which is a higher spiritual understanding and organization and systematization of knowledge and (its) application, than what was readily available; either *verbatim* within the literary tradition at Grade-II, or within even the *common* understanding of "magic" and "mysticism."

So, we're dealing with the *secrets*—at Grade-III we're dealing with upper-level secrets of, essentially, any and all of these "Ancient Mystery Schools," "Secret Societies," traditions, cabals, you know, fraternities and so forth; because this is what they've all been leaning towards or seeking to access as a point *beyond* "physical existence." Of course, many of them have not—well, nearly all of them at this point; we don't know of any that have actually pierced these veils up until the work that we've been recently doing—and we've been doing it, leaning on the shoulders of 6,000 of evolution of human civilization of efforts and attempts in this direction; so, it isn't as if we are spawning this from nothing. Okay? But we are already working at—and have already taken—a Master-Level examination of everything that has come before; and after being able to do that, well, *what's keeping us from going forward?*

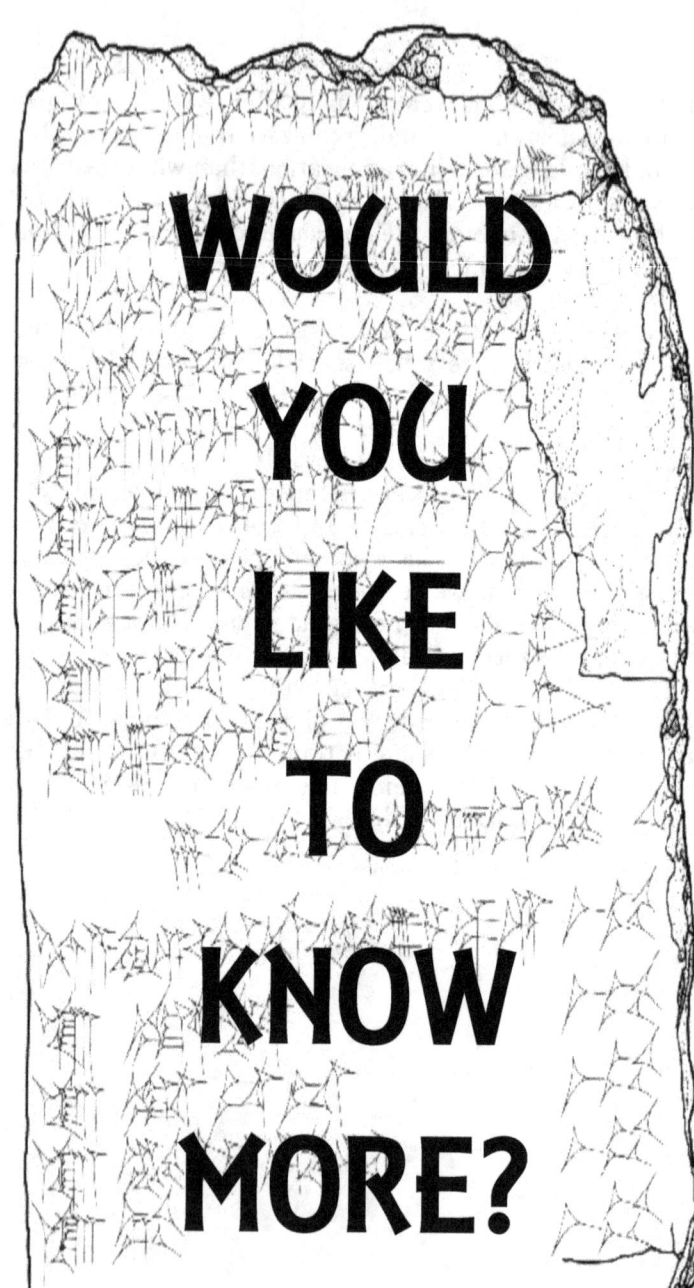

AVAILABLE FROM THE **JOSHUA FREE** PUBLISHING IMPRINT

The Original Mardukite Master Course Lecture Volumes!
Experience the Legendary Course from anywhere
in the Universe – Available in four volumes!

MAGICK & MYSTICISM
The Academy Lectures – Vol. I

DRUIDS, ELVES & DRAGONS
The Academy Lectures – Vol. II

Based on the lectures by Joshua Free

Transcripts of the Mardukite Master Course Academy Lectures given at the Mardukite Academy in September 2020.

This is part of a four-part series, each volume providing a serious Seeker with transcripts to 12 of the 48 Academy Lectures previously published in the mega-anthology "*Complete Mardukite Master Course.*" Each volume is designed to match the correlating Master Edition textbook, such as "Great Magickal Arcanum," "Merlyn's Complete Book of Druidism," "Necronomicon: The Complete Anunnaki Legacy" and "Systemology Handbook."

AVAILABLE FROM THE **JOSHUA FREE** PUBLISHING IMPRINT

*The Original Classic Underground Bestseller Returns!
10th Anniversary Hardcover Collector's Edition.
Explore the original religion on Earth.*

SUMERIAN RELIGION
Introducing the Anunnaki Gods
of Mesopotamian Neopaganism

by Joshua Free

*Develop a personal relationship with Anunnaki Gods
—the divine pantheon that launched a thousand
cultures and traditions throughout the world!*

Even if you think you already know all about the Sumerian Anunnaki or Star-Gates of Babylon... ∗ Here you will find a beautifully crafted journey that is unlike anything Humans have had the opportunity to experience for thousands of years... ∗ Here you will find a truly remarkable tome demonstrating a fresh new approach to modern Mesopotamian Neopaganism and spirituality... ∗ Here is a Master Key to the ancient mystic arts: true knowledge concerning the powers and entities that these arts are dedicated to... ∗ A working relationship with these powers directly... ∗ And wisdom to exist "alongside" the gods, ever to remain in the "favor" of Cosmic Law. The original precursor to *"Babylonian Myth & Magic."*

(*Mardukite Research, Grade-II Zuism, Liber-50*)

AVAILABLE FROM THE **JOSHUA FREE** PUBLISHING IMPRINT

THE COMPLETE BOOK OF MARDUK BY NABU

A Pocket Anunnaki Devotional Companion to Babylonian Rituals

edited by Joshua Free

10th Anniversary
Collector's Edition Hardcover

Mardukite Liber-W
Grade-II Zuism

THE MAQLU RITUAL BOOK

A Pocket Companion to Babylonian Exorcisms, Banishing Rites & Protective Spells

edited by Joshua Free

10th Anniversary
Collector's Edition Hardcover

Mardukite Liber-M
Grade-II Zuism

AVAILABLE FROM THE **JOSHUA FREE** PUBLISHING IMPRINT

SYSTEMOLOGY
The Pathway to Self-Honesty

A Concise Introduction to Mardukite Systemology

THE WAY INTO THE
FUTURE

A Handbook for the New Human

a collection of writings by
Joshua Free
as selected by James Thomas

now available as a Collector's Edition Hardcover

Here are the basic answers to what has held Humanity back from achieving its ultimate goals and unlocking the true power of the Spirit and highest state of Knowing and Being.

"The Way Into The Future" illuminates the *Pathway* leading to Planet Earth's true "metahuman" destiny. With *excerpts from "Tablets of Destiny," "Crystal Clear," "Systemology—Original Thesis"* and *"The Power of Zu."* You can help shine clear light on anyone's pathway!

Carefully selected by Mardukite Publications Officer, James Thomas, this critical *collection of eighteen articles, lecture transcripts and reference chapters* by Joshua Free is sure to be not only a treasured part of your personal library, but also the perfect introduction for all friends, family and loved ones.

(Basic Grade-III Introductory Pocket Anthology)

AVAILABLE FROM THE **JOSHUA FREE** PUBLISHING IMPRINT

SYSTEMOLOGY
The Pathway to Self-Honesty

ORIGINAL UNDERGROUND INTRODUCTIONS
REVISED AND REISSUED IN HARDCOVER

SYSTEMOLOGY
The Original Thesis of Mardukite New Thuoght

by Joshua Free

(*Mardukite Systemology Liber-S-1X*)

The very first underground discourses released to the "New Thought" division of the Mardukite Research Organization privately over a decade ago and providing the inspiration for rapid futurist spiritual technology called "Mardukite Systemology."

THE POWER OF ZU
Applying Mardukite Zuism & Systemology to Everyday Life

by Joshua Free
Foreword by Reed Penn

(*Mardukite Systemology Liber-S-1Z*)

A unique introductory course on Mardukite Zuism & Systemology, including transcripts from a 3-day lecture series given by Joshua Free in December 2019 to launch the Mardukite Academy of Systemology & Founding Church of Mardukite Zuism just in time for the 2020's.

AVAILABLE FROM THE **JOSHUA FREE** PUBLISHING IMPRINT

The Ultimate Necronomicon of the 21st Century!
Hardcover! Nearly 1000 Pages!

NECRONOMICON:
THE COMPLETE ANUNNAKI LEGACY
(*Complete Grade-II Master Edition Anthology*)
collected works by Joshua Free

And don't miss the newly released portable abridgment
of the original "Anunnaki Bible" scriptural edition...

ANUNNAKI BIBLE

THE CUNEIFORM SCRIPTURES
NEW STANDARD ZUIST EDITION

Premiere Founders Edition for
Church of Mardukite Zuism

edited by Joshua Free

Premiere Edition Hardcover
and
Pocket Paperback Available

WOULD YOU LIKE TO KNOW MORE ???

Take your first steps on the

SYSTEMOLOGY
Pathway to Self-Honesty

with the book that started it all!

Rediscover the original system of perfecting the Human Condition on a Pathway that leads to Infinity. Here is a way!—a map to chart spiritual potential and redefine the future of what it means to be human.

A landmark public debut of Grade-III Systemology and foundation stone for reaching higher and taking back control of your

DESTINY

(Mardukite Systemology Grade-III Research Volume, Liber-One)

AVAILABLE FROM THE **JOSHUA FREE** PUBLISHING IMPRINT

SYSTEMOLOGY
The Pathway to Self-Honesty

CRYSTAL CLEAR

(Handbook for Seekers)

Self-Actualization and Spiritual Ascension in This Lifetime

by Joshua Free

Mardukite Systemology Grade-III, Liber-2B

Revised Edition

available exclusively as an Academy Edition Collector's Hardcover

Take control of your destiny and chart the first steps toward your own spiritual evolution.
Realize new potentials of the Human Condition with a Self-guiding handbook for Self-Processing toward Self-Actualization in Self-Honesty using actual techniques and training provided for the coveted "Mardukite Self-Defragmentation Course Program" —once only available directly and privately from the underground International Systemology Society.

Discover the amazing power behind the applied spiritual technology used for counseling and advisement in the Mardukite Zuism tradition.

(Revised Second Edition Now Available!)

AVAILABLE FROM THE **JOSHUA FREE** PUBLISHING IMPRINT

SYSTEMOLOGY
The Pathway to Self-Honesty

SYSTEMOLOGY HANDBOOK

The ultimate operator's manual to the Human Condition and unlocking the true power of the Spirit.

** *"Modern Mardukite Zuism"* **
** *"The Tablets of Destiny"* **
** *"Crystal Clear"* **
** *"The Power of ZU"* **
** *"Systemology—Original Thesis"* **
** *Human, More Than Human* **
** *Defragmentation* **
** *Patterns & Cycles* **
** *Transhuman Generations* **

(Complete Grade-III Master Edition Anthology)

AVAILABLE FROM THE **JOSHUA FREE** PUBLISHING IMPRINT

MARDUKITE MASTER COURSE
Keys to the Gates of Higher Understanding

Now you can experience the Legendary "Master Course" from anywhere in the Universe, exactly as given in person by Joshua Free to the "Mardukite Academy of Systemology" in September 2020.

800+ pages of materials collected in this volume provide Seekers with full transcripts to all *48 Academy Lectures* of the legendary "*Mardukite Master Course*" combined with all course outlines, supplements and critical handouts from the original "*Instructor's Manual*"—making this the most complete definitive single-source delivery of New Age understanding and spiritual technology.

Referencing 25 years of research, development and publishing, including "*Necronomicon: The Complete Anunnaki Legacy,*" "*The Great Magickal Arcanum,*" "*The Systemology Handbook*" and "*Merlyn's Complete Book of Druidism.*"

AVAILABLE FROM THE **JOSHUA FREE** PUBLISHING IMPRINT

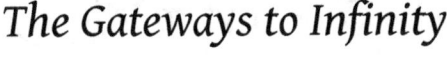

The Gateways to Infinity

METAHUMAN DESTINATIONS

Piloting the Course to Homo Novus

Written by Joshua Free
Foreword by David Zibert

Mardukite Systemology Grade-IV Metahumanism Professional Pilot Course, Liber-Two

exclusively available in a hardcover premiere first edition

Drawing from the "Arcane Tablets" and nearly a year of additional research, experimentation and workshops since the introduction of applied spiritual technology and systematic processing methods, Joshua Free provides the ground-breaking manual for those seeking to correct—or "defragment"—the conditions that have trapped viewpoints of the Spirit into programming and encoding of the Human Condition.

Experience the revolutionary professional course in advanced spiritual technology for Mardukite Systemologists to "Pilot" the way to higher ideals that can free us from the Human Condition and return ultimate command and control of creation to the Spirit.

(Includes Grade-IV Liber-2C, Liber-2D and Liber-3C)

AVAILABLE FROM THE **JOSHUA FREE** PUBLISHING IMPRINT

SYSTEMOLOGY
The Gateways to Infinity

IMAGINOMICON

Accessing the Gateway to Higher Universes

A New Grimoire for the Human Spirit

by Joshua Free

Mardukite Systemology Grade-IV Metahumanism, Wizard Level-0, Liber-3D

available in both as premiere hardcover or revised collector's edition

The Way Out. Hidden for 6,000 Years.
But now we've found the Key.
A grimore to summon and invoke, command and control,
the most powerful spirit to ever exist.
Your Self.

Access beyond physical existence.
Fly free across all Gateways.
Go back to where it all began and reclaim that
personal universe which the *Spirit* once called "*Home.*"

Break free from the Matrix;
control the Mind and command the Body
from outside those systems
— because *You* were never "human" —
fully realize what it means to be a *spiritual being*,
then rise up through the Gateways to Higher Universes
and *BE.*

AVAILABLE FROM THE **JOSHUA FREE** PUBLISHING IMPRINT

*Original underground classics.
Joshua Free's bestselling
"Druid Trilogy"*

DRACONOMICON
The Book of Ancient Dragon Magick
25th Anniversary Hardcover
Collector's Edition
by Joshua Free

THE DRUID'S HANDBOOK
Ancient Magick for a New Age
20th Anniversary Hardcover
Collector's Edition
by Joshua Free

ELVENOMICON -or- SECRET TRADITIONS OF ELVES AND FAERIES
The Book of Elven Magick
& Druid Lore
15th Anniversary Hardcover
Collector's Edition
by Joshua Free

*All three Grade-I Route-D titles
(...plus additional material...)
now available in the anthology:*
***Merlyn's Complete
Book of Druidism***
by Joshua Free.

AVAILABLE FROM THE **JOSHUA FREE** PUBLISHING IMPRINT

SYSTEMOLOGY
Gateways to Infinite Self-Honesty

THE WAY OF THE WIZARD
(Utilitarian Systemology)
A New Metahuman Ethic
by Joshua Free

The Systemology Society Beta-Defragmentation Booster
and stabilizer for upper-level Wizard Grades.
Based on the "Freedom From" Grade-IV lecture series
given by Joshua Free in July 2021 at Mardukite Academy
and developmental research for the remaining year.

Accumulated involvement in dangerous situations, states of
confusion, unjust destruction and being at the effect end of faulty
—or blatantly false—information, all lend to fragmented purposes
that are non-survival (or counter-survival) oriented, leading us
away from routes to achieve "greater heights"—higher more ideal
states of Knowing and Beingness—including the
"Magic Universe" preceding this one.

(Mardukite Systemology Grade-IV-V Bridge, Liber-Three/3E)

THE MARDUKITE RESEARCH LIBRARY ARCHIVE COLLECTION

AVAILABLE FROM THE **JOSHUA FREE** PUBLISHING IMPRINT

Necronomicon: The Anunnaki Bible : 10th Anniversary Collector's Edition—LIBER-N,L,G,9+W-M+S *(Hardcover)*

Gates of the Necronomicon : The Secret Anunnaki Tradition of Babylon : 10th Anniversary Collector's Edition—LIBER-50,51/52,R+555 *(Hardcover)*

Necronomicon—The Anunnaki Grimoire : A Manual of Practical Babylonian Magick : 10th Anniversary Collector's Edition—LIBER-E,W/Z,M+K *(Hardcover)*

The Complete Anunnaki Bible: A Source Book of Esoteric Archaeology—LIBER-N,L,G,9+W-M+S *(Hardcover and Paperback)*

Anunnaki Bible : The Cuneiform Scriptures—New Standard Zuist Edition : Abridged Pocket Version *(Hardcover & Paperback)*

Sumerian Religion : Introducing the Anunnaki Gods of Mesopotamian Neopaganism : 10th Anniv. Collector's Ed.—LIBER-50 *(Hardcover)*

Babylonian Myth & Magic : Anunnaki Mysticism of Mesopotamian Neopaganism : 10th Anniv. Coll. Ed.—LIBER-51+E *(Hardcover)*

The Complete Book of Marduk by Nabu : A Pocket Anunnaki Devotional Companion to Babylonian Prayers & Rituals : 10th Anniversary Collector's Edition—LIBER-W+Z *(Hardcover)*

The Maqlu Ritual Book : A Pocket Companion to Babylonian Exorcisms, Banishing Rites & Protective Spells : 10th Anniversary Collector's Edition—LIBER-M *(Hardcover)*

Novem Portis: Necronomicon Revelations & Nine Gates of the Kingdom of Shadows : 10th Anniv. Collector's Ed.—LIBER-R+9 *(Hardcover)*

Elvenomicon—or—Secret Traditions of Elves & Faeries : Elven Magick & Druid Lore : 15th Anniv. Collector's Ed.—LIBER-D *(Hardcover)*

Draconomicon : The Book of Ancient Dragon Magick 25th Anniversary Collector's Edition—LIBER-D3 *(Hardcover)*

The Druid's Handbook : Ancient Magick for a New Age 20th Anniversary Collector's Edition—LIBER-D2 *(Hardcover)*

The Sorcerer's Handbook : A Complete Guide to Practical Magick 21st Anniversary Collector's Edition—*(Hardcover)*

The Witch's Handbook : A Complete Grimoire of Witchcraft 21st Anniversary Collector's Edition—*(Hardcover)*

The Vampyre's Handbook : Secret Rites of Modern Vampires 5th Anniversary Collector's Edition—LIBER V1+V2 *(Hardcover)*

∞

SILVER ANNIVERSARY
19 95 — 20 20
JOSHUA FREE

PUBLISHED BY THE **JOSHUA FREE** IMPRINT REPRESENTING

**The Founding Church of Mardukite Zuism
& Mardukite Academy of Systemology**

mardukite.com

www.ingramcontent.com/pod-product-compliance
Lightning Source LLC
Chambersburg PA
CBHW050331010526
44119CB00004B/118